IRAN'S EMISSARIES
of
TERROR

How mullahs' embassies run the network of espionage and murder

Published by

**National Council of Resistance of Iran
U.S. Representative Office (NCRI-US)**

Iran's Emissaries of Terror;
How mullahs' embassies run the network of espionage and murder

First published in 2019 by
National Council of Resistance of Iran — U.S. Representative Office (NCRI-US),
1747 Pennsylvania Ave., NW, Suite 1125, Washington, DC 20006

ISBN-10 (hard cover): 1-944942-27-0
ISBN-13 (hard cover): 978-1-944942-27-4

ISBN-10 (paperback): 1-944942-25-4
ISBN-13 (paperback): 978-1-944942-25-0

ISBN-10 (e-book): 1-944942-26-2
ISBN-13 (e-book): 978-1-944942-26-7

Library of Congress Control Number: 2019938405

Library of Congress Cataloging-in-Publication Data

National Council of Resistance of Iran - U.S. Representative Office.
Iran's Emissaries of Terror; How mullahs' embassies run the network of espionage and murder

1. Iran. 2. Terrorism. 3. Diplomacy. 4. Europe. 5. Middle East

First Edition: May 2019
Printed in the United States of America

These materials are being distributed by the National Council of Resistance of Iran-U.S. Representative Office. Additional information is on file with the Department of Justice, Washington, D.C.

Table of Contents

Summary

In July 2018, Assadollah Assadi, a high-ranking Iranian diplomat based in Austria, was arrested in Germany and charged with masterminding, directing and providing resources and explosives to bomb a large gathering of the Iranian opposition held by the National Council of Resistance of Iran (NCRI) in Villepinte, a suburb of Paris. In March 2018, Tehran's diplomats in Albania, including its ambassador, engineered a truck-bombing attack against the residence of 2,500 members and leaders of the People's Mojahedin Organization of Iran (PMOI), also known as *Mujahedin-e-Khalq-Iran* (MEK), near Tirana.

Thankfully, these terror plots were neutralized hours before the planned explosions, but they served as a wakeup call for Europe and the U.S. The world came to realize the extent to which Tehran's embassies and diplomats are at the core of both the planning and execution of terrorism targeting Iranian dissidents, as well as central to Tehran's direct and proxy terrorism against other countries.

The escalation of terrorist acts in 2018 targeting the MEK, as the leading organized opposition, and the NCRI coalition to which it belongs, is directly linked to the broad-based revolt in Iran's streets which has been ongoing since December 2017. While crushing economic hardships and rampant poverty caused by corrupt and inept leadership are powerful catalysts, Supreme Leader Ali Khamenei has explicitly identified the MEK as the organizer of the nationwide uprising and has publicly vowed to eliminate them.

Alarmed at its predicament, the regime devised a three-pronged strategy to organizationally and politically render the MEK ineffective in the hope of curtailing the uprising. The first component of Tehran's anti-MEK playbook is a campaign of arrests and even murders of MEK activists and protesters. In a report entitled "Iran's 'year of shame,'" Amnesty International stated that more than 7,000 had been "arrested in a chilling crackdown on dissent during 2018."

The second component is to escalate the demonization campaign, directly or through intermediaries, and spread misinformation and falsehoods vilifying the MEK.

The third element of this strategy, and the focus of this book, is Tehran's escalation of terrorist operations to eradicate the leadership and rank-and-file of the NCRI and MEK, and their supporters. To this end, Tehran's embassies and consulates serve as hubs, while its diplomats act as controllers and operatives.

While terrorism has always been at the core of Iran's foreign policy and an extension of its domestic suppression of dissidents, a convenient fallacy that such malign acts are the work of a few rogue elements or a dissenting faction inside the regime has prevented the world from forming a united front to confront the terrorism. In reality, the government-sponsored acts of terror are facilitated, financed and directed at the highest levels of the regime, with the authorization of Supreme Leader Ali Khamenei himself. A surreptitious unit reporting directly to Khamenei called the Special Affairs Office of the Supreme Leader is at the apex of the pyramid of agencies which make up the terror apparatus. These agencies include the Supreme National Security Council (SNSC), Ministry of Intelligence and Security (MOIS), and the Islamic Revolutionary Guards Corp's (IRGC) Quds Force and Intelligence Organization.

Over the years, many of the field operatives and directors of the assassinations and terror bombings have been placed in top government positions and promoted to influential levels of power within the regime's intelligence and security organs in both the so-called "moderate" and "hardline" administrations, including that of Hassan Rouhani.

Not surprisingly, the surge in Tehran's terror and espionage on Western soil has prompted some, albeit relatively soft, diplomatic and law enforcement response. In 2018 alone, five Iranian diplomats, including an ambassador, were expelled; one senior intelligence-agent-turned-diplomat is in prison; and dozens of agents were arrested in Europe and the United States — all on terrorism and espionage-related charges.

There has also been an intensified conversation in Western capitals on the need for pragmatic, effective and pro-active measures and policy to counter the regime's terrorism around the world. Such measures need to be swiftly and effectively implemented.

The overarching component of such a policy should be recognition of the inalienable and legitimate right of Iranian people to overthrow the theocratic regime. There is global consensus that Tehran's unbridled terrorism and the plethora of its other malign conduct are by-products of its fundamentalist, suppressive, and expansionist nature.

Among the specific recommendations critical to a worthwhile counter-terrorism policy are that as a follow up to the long-overdue FTO designation of the IRGC, the MOIS be similarly designated by the U.S., and blacklisted by Europe; Iran's terrorist-diplomats be expelled; and the agents of its intelligence services be prosecuted and/or expelled from the U.S. and Europe.

Introduction

Modern global terrorism has been predominantly shaped and defined by the Islamic Republic of Iran. Since its inception, Iran's theocratic dictatorship has maintained its hold on power essentially by two means: internal repression and the spread of extremism and terrorism abroad. Understanding the connection between these two is key to understanding Tehran's motives and tactics in its execution of terrorism outside Iran's borders.

As the legitimacy of Iran's ruling regime began to wane among Iranians soon after the 1979 Revolution, it had to resort to violent suppression of the democratic secular opposition to maintain control. Meanwhile, the driving force of its terrorism outside Iran shifted from ideological to transactional, i.e. terror as leverage and diplomacy. Starting in the late 1980s and early 1990s, the regime also began using the newly formed Quds Force to assassinate and kidnap opposition figures abroad.

In this malevolent evolution, the web of intelligence agencies has taken over Tehran's embassies, positioning their most effective agents as high-level, accredited diplomats. These emissaries of terror are the architects and operatives of terror plots to reinforce Tehran's diplomacy and eliminate Iranian dissidents in exile. Exploiting the expansive network of the diplomatic apparatus, including hundreds of embassies, consulates, and cultural and religious centers, Tehran's terrorists have effective reach abroad under the protective cover of diplomatic immunity.

The July 2018 arrest in Germany of Assadollah Assadi, a Vienna-based senior diplomat, on charges of masterminding a plot to bomb the 100,000-strong "Iran Freedom" gathering held by the National Council of Resistance of Iran (NCRI) near Paris, preceded by the March 2018 bombing plot by Iran's top diplomat in Albania against a facility of the opposition *Mujahedin-e Khalq* (MEK), once again brought the role of Iran's diplomatic facilities and personnel into the spotlight.

Are these emissaries of terror acting autonomously? Are they rogue elements or a dissenting faction inside the regime hoping to undermine its "moderate" president, Hassan Rouhani? Such Tehran-friendly fallacies are refuted by the predominance of field operatives and directors of the assassinations and terror bombings in top government positions.

The more pertinent question is, why would Tehran risk intense diplomatic, political, and security fall out, and opt to go ahead with such audacious plots, potentially injuring or killing not just its opposition, but also hundreds of international guests, including current and former U.S. and European officials? And why would it do so in the heart of Europe, when it vitally needs European support and engagement? Why risk so much of its fast-dwindling political capital to attack the MEK opposition movement, which, according to the regime's PR machine and its western mouthpieces, has "no support inside the country"?

The answers lie in how all this relates to the nationwide anti-regime unrest which erupted in late December 2017, spreading to nearly 160 towns and cities. The role of the MEK in the intensity and resilience of the protests, undeniably an existential threat for the ruling regime, and the rising domestic and international prominence of the NCRI as the viable alternative, are driving the surge in Tehran's domestic suppression, demonization campaign, and terror and espionage operations targeting the MEK in Europe and the United States.

What are the policy implications and diplomatic consequences of the regime's formula for survival, i.e. utilizing intelligence agents and assassins posing as diplomats to eradicate its main opposition, and in the process bring death, destruction and disorder to Western soil?

In the early 1990s, the National Council of Resistance of Iran warned the free world that the Islamic fundamentalism emanating from Tehran was "the new global threat." Tehran, then and now, is committed to using terrorism, directly or by proxy, to export what it calls the "Islamic Revolution." From Iraq to Yemen, and from Lebanon to Syria, hundreds of thousands have died and cities have been destroyed. Embassies, military barracks, cultural and community centers have been bombed, passenger airlines hijacked, civilian and governmental figures kidnapped and murdered. Stopping or even diminishing the clerical regime's capacity for terrorism will go a long way toward reducing insecurity and mayhem in the Middle East and beyond.

The connection between Tehran's application of internal suppression and external terrorism at those critical junctures when its survival is in jeopardy, is markedly evident in its targeting of the leading democratic opposition. This book briefly addresses this topic and others mentioned above in order to contribute to discussions on a meaningful policy to curb the Iranian regime's network of espionage, terrorism and murder.

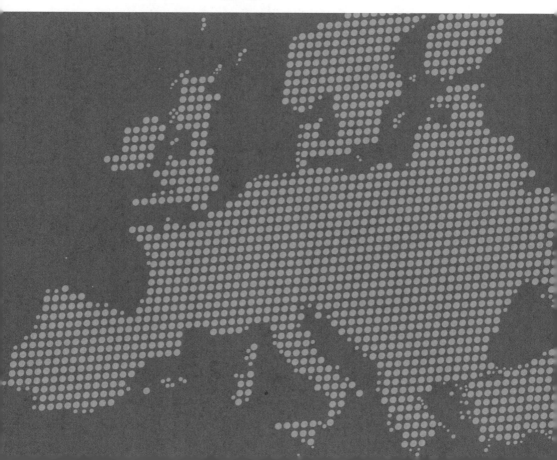

Chapter One

A Moribund Regime Resorts to Terrorism to Target Its Opposition

In late 2017 and early 2018, nationwide protests erupted in Iran. In over 160 towns and cities, the Iranian people rose up, demanding the clerical regime's overthrow. Shaken to its core, Tehran's ruling elite has been frantically trying in the ensuing months to suppress the uprising, albeit unsuccessfully. Unrest, harshly suppressed in one town or city, flares up elsewhere. In the meantime, the clerical regime has exhibited little or no solutions to address the Iranian people's needs. Today, any economic or social grievance promptly leads to the same conclusion: The solution is to topple the regime.

"All of a sudden, the country's climate changed," a stunned Hassan Rouhani, complained to the *Majlis* (parliament) on August 28. "The slogans gradually ... turned into structure-shattering slogans. ... Such an incident was rare in all the previous years."[1]

Regime's President Hassan Rouhani: The slogans gradually... turned into structure shattering slogans.

Tehran's president was understandably taken aback by the depth, breadth, and resilience of the protests, which have evolved into an existential threat. Iran's people are demanding an alternative to four decades of corruption, mis-management and theocratic intolerance, demands which Tehran's leaders are neither willing nor able to meet. Instead, they view their best option as striking out at the organized opposition and alternative, the People's Mojahedin Organization of Iran (PMOI), also known by its Farsi name *Mujaheddin-e-Khalq-*

e-Iran (MEK), and the opposition coalition to which it belongs, the National Council of Resistance of Iran (NCRI). They point to the urgency and gravity of the situation, and the MEK's role in directing and advancing the uprisings.

Regime's Supreme Leader Ali Khamenei: the uprising was organized by the MEK, who had planned for it for months.

On January 9, Supreme Leader Ali Khamenei stressed that the uprising was being organized by the MEK, who had planned for it for months. He threatened that "this effort will not remain without consequences."[2]

At the height of anti-government protests in January 2018, in an embarrassing move for a regime which boasts of being the region's powerhouse, Rouhani reached out to his French counterpart. In an hour-long telephone conversation with Emmanuel Macron, Rouhani urged the French president to adopt practical measures restricting activities by the MEK in France. Macron declined.[3]

Within the first week of unrest in December 2017, the Secretary of the Supreme National Security Council, Ali Shamkhani, said, the goal of organized foreign intervention is to prevent progress in Iran, and therefore, they are trying to bring about the collapse of the country from within.

In the context of the nationwide unrest as a threat to its survival, the regime's cost-benefit analysis deems any diplomatic price or consequence resulting from extreme measures as acceptable. In Shamkhani's words, the MEK "will get the appropriate response from whence they know not."

Upsurge in terrorist operations in the West

In recent years, specifically following the signing of the nuclear deal (Joint Comprehensive Plan of Action, JCPOA), the clerical regime exploited the West's appeasement policy to expand its terrorist operations in Europe and the U.S. 2018 saw an upsurge of terror operations against dissidents. Outlined in the table below, ten terror plots took place in the U.S., France, Albania, Germany, Belgium, the UK, the Netherlands, and Turkey.

Date	Country	Description
December 14, 2018	Albania	Albanian Government expels Tehran's ambassador and another MOIS agent for terrorism plots.
October 30, 2018	Denmark	Danish authorities reveal that Tehran was behind a conspiracy to assassinate an Iranian-Arab in Denmark. A Norwegian-Iranian, a longtime agent of the MOIS in Norway, was arrested and charged with complicity.

Date	Country	Description
Aug. 9, 2018	U.S.A.	Two Iranians, Ahmadreza Mohammadi-Doostdar, 38, and Majid Ghorbani, 59, were arrested by the FBI in the United States. They were gathering intelligence for the regime's Ministry of Intelligence and Security (MOIS).
June 30, 2018	France	MOIS set in motion a sophisticated terrorist plot involving its diplomat-terrorists, including Assadollah Assadi stationed in its embassy in Austria, and several other individuals. The plot aimed to detonate a bomb at the MEK rally in Villepinte near Paris. The scheme was neutralized through the efforts of Belgian, German and French police. Those involved were arrested.
June 2018	The Netherlands	The Dutch security office expelled two Iranian diplomats in June 2018 in connection with terrorist acts of the Iranian regime in the Netherlands. Ahmad Mola Nissi, a leader of the al-Ahvazieh Movement, was shot dead in front of his house by an assailant armed with a gun equipped with a silencer.

Date	Country	Description
Mar. 22, 2018	Albania	MOIS plotted to set off a truck bomb near a hall where a Persian New Year celebration was being held. Two regime agents who had entered Albania posing as reporters were arrested and the conspiracy was neutralized.
Feb. 5, 2018	Turkey	Arash Shoja Shargh, a dissident journalist, disappeared in Van, a city in central Turkey.
Jan. 16, 2018	Germany	On the orders of the German Federal Prosecutor's Office, German special forces raided the homes and centers of 10 spies and agents tied to the IRGC's Quds Force residing in various German provinces, leading to their arrests. The investigations were conducted in the states of Berlin, Württemberg, Baden, Bayern, and North Rhine Westphalia.
Jan. 16, 2018	Germany	Espionage targeting a former head of a German-Israeli association by a 10-person team of the regime's terrorists continued for two years until 2018. The plot was uncovered by German police.
Jan. 11, 2018	Britain	A terrorist plot against Mahmoud Ahmad, an Ahvazi activist, was foiled.

Tehran sets its sights on MEK in Albania

In the aftermath of rocket attacks on their camps and the massacre of MEK members by Iran regime's agents in Iraq, in May 2013 the government of Albania began accepting MEK members as refugees. Shortly thereafter, the regime's Ministry of Intelligence and Security (MOIS) began sending its agents to the embassy in Tirana. In subsequent months and years, the mullahs' embassy in Albania has become one of the most important Iranian embassies in Europe.

A year after being tasked to head the intelligence station at the embassy in Albania, Mostafa Roudaki, a senior MOIS officer, masterminded a major terror plot against the facility housing more than 2,500 MEK members on the eve of the Iranian New Year celebration (*Nowruz*) in March 2018.

Newly-constructed MEK facility, Ashraf III, in Tirana, Albania

Similar to the operations that ISIS has carried out in terms of targeting big crowds and inflicting damage to a large number of people at once, the terrorists planned to use a truck bomb to blow up a large gathering attended by the leadership of the Iranian Resistance, including NCRI President-elect Maryam Rajavi. The audience included many NCRI members, the General Secretary and Leadership Council of the MEK, as well as VIPs from the U.S. such as Mayor Rudy Giuliani, and from Albania, such as, Pandeli Majko, former Prime Minister and current Minister of Diasporas.

Thankfully, the plot was foiled in time by the security services of Albania,[4] who arrested two regime agents who had entered Albania posing as reporters. The U.S. Department of State reported that two Iranian agents had been arrested on terrorism charges by Albanian authorities on March 22.[5] In April, Prime Minister Eddie Rama emphasized that the Albanian government along with other European countries was taking action against the terrorist threat posed by Tehran.[6]

> Similar to the operations that ISIS has carried out the terrorists planned to use a truck bomb to blow up a large gathering attended by the leadership of the Iranian Resistance

2018 Nowruz celebrations in Ashraf III, Albania where dozens of international VIPs and thousands of MEK leadership and members attended.

In an interview with Fox News on August 9, 2018, former Prime Minister Majko said that "U.S. officials have told him that due to information on threats against him, he should increase his protection. He added that Iran's strategy in the region is unprecedented."[7]

On August 13, 2018, in a letter to Edi Rama, Prime Minister of Albania, Congressman Ted Poe (R-TX) wrote:

> *As you are likely aware, European security authorities recently arrested 2 Iranian-Belgians for attempting to blow up the Free Iran 2018 gathering in Paris, France. My office is particularly concerned for the safety of the Mojahedin-e-Khalgh (MEK) members now living in your country because European police have detained and charged Asadollah Assadi, the Vienna station chief of Iran's Ministry of Intelligence*

and Security, for providing the bomb detonators to these terrorists.

For decades, Iran has been a leading state sponsor of terrorism, but the aforementioned Iranian diplomat's direct involvement in the plot to bomb a rally in which thousands of American citizens participated, truly crosses a line.

In addition to terrorism in Western Europe, the Iranian embassy in Albania has increasingly been active and cited by U.S, Department of State for planning terrorist attacks, potentially including those targeting the MEK. Iranian terrorist networks in the Balkans are expanding and the regime's funding of extremist groups and unsuspecting organizations is a source of great concern.

I therefore urge your continued vigilance and ask you to ensure adequate security measures are in place to counter Iranian terrorist threats and infrastructure — to protect innocent Albanians as well the MEK members living in your country.

On August 20, 2018, a bipartisan group of members of the U.S. Congress wrote to Prime Minister Rama to "express our concern about the security risk Iranian regime-sponsored terrorism presents for the people and country of Albania. We believe that with the imposition of additional international pressure and increased anti-regime protests, Iran is targeting the Mojahedine Khalgh (MEK) members living in Albania and beyond."

The congressional letter added:

According to the State Department, in March 2018, your country's intelligence service arrested two Iranian nationals, suspected to be agents of the Iranian regime targeting the MEK, for planning acts of terrorism. Additionally, Belgian, French, and German intelligence foiled an Iran-sponsored terror plot to bomb an MEK event in June 2018 in Paris and arrested two Iranians, as well as a senior Iranian diplomat (Asadollah Assadi). Assadi has since been stripped of diplomatic immunity and charged in both Germany and Belgium. Furthermore, the diplomat whom Assadi had replaced in Vienna (Mostafa Roudaki) now works in a similar role at the Iranian embassy in Tirana, Albania.

These arrests in the Balkans and other parts of Europe point to the Iranian regime's malign activities in Europe, including Albania, which demand our heightened vigilance and attention. The security of Albania, as a friend of the United States, is critical. Accordingly, we urge you to take necessary measures to stop malign activities of the Iranian regime in Albania, and seriously consider restricting the Iranian regime's presence in Albania under diplomatic pretexts.

23

On December 19, 2018, Albania's Foreign Ministry announced that the regime's Ambassador and another Tehran diplomat had been expelled for "involvement in activities harmful to national security." The two expelled diplomats, Gholamhossein Mohammadnia, the regime's ambassador, and Mostafa Roudaki, the first consul, are both high-ranking intelligence agents.

Albanian Foreign Ministry spokeswoman Edlira Prendi told reporters on December 20 that the "activities of these two diplomats were contrary to diplomatic protocol," adding that Tirana had made the decision to declare them *persona non grata* in consultation with other countries.[8]

On December 19, the diplomatic mission of the United States published an official letter to the Albanian prime minister signed by President Donald Trump, dated December 14, in which the U.S. president congratulated Albania for taking the step and thanking the Albanian Prime Minister for his government's "steadfast efforts to stand up to Iran and to counter destabilizing activities and efforts to silence dissidents around the globe."[11]

THE WHITE HOUSE

WASHINGTON

December 14, 2018

His Excellency
Edi Rama
Prime Minister of the Republic of Albania
Tirana

Dear Mr. Prime Minister:

Thank you for your steadfast efforts to stand up to Iran and to counter its destabilizing activities and efforts to silence dissidents around the globe. The leadership you have shown by expelling Iran's Ambassador to your country exemplifies our joint efforts to show the Iranian government that its terrorist activities in Europe and around the world will have severe consequences.

Albania has always been a great friend to the United States, and I look forward to growing our partnership as we confront the many important issues facing our two countries.

Sincerely,

President Donald Trump's December 14, 2018 official letter to the Albanian prime minister.

U.S. Secretary of State Mike Pompeo commended the Albanian prime minister's decision to expel "two Iranian agents who plotted terrorist attacks in Albania."[9] U.S. national security advisor John Bolton also said in a tweet: "Prime Minister Edi Rama of Albania just expelled the Iranian ambassador, signaling to Iran's leaders that their support for terrorism will not be tolerated."[10]

Secretary Mike Pompeo praised Albania for expulsion of "two Iranian agents who plotted terrorist attacks."

Prime Minister Edi Rama of Albania just expelled the Iranian ambassador, signaling to Iran's leaders that their support for terrorism will not be tolerated. We stand with PM Rama and the Albanian people as they stand up to Iran's reckless behavior in Europe and across the globe.

3:55 PM - 19 Dec 2018

National Security Advisor Amb. John Bolton's tweet on expulsion of regime's agents from Albania

Bomb plot against Resistance rally in Paris

Another terrorist scheme to bomb a large gathering of the Iranian Resistance, this time in Villepinte, a suburb of Paris, was neutralized hours before the planned explosion on June 30, 2018. Tens of thousands of Iranian expatriates were joined at the Paris rally by nearly 600 political dignitaries from close to 70 countries, including the U.S., Europe and the Middle East.[12]

Citing analysis provided by Western as well as Middle Eastern intelligence and security officials and analysts, the *Washington Post* reported that the regime's leaders — under

As many as 100,000 Iranian expatriates were joined at the Paris Free Iran gathering by nearly 600 political dignitaries from close to 70 countries, including the U.S., Europe and the Middle East, June 30, 2018.

100,000 participants attend the 2018 Paris Free Iran gathering which was the target of a foiled massive bomb plot by Tehran.

internal and external pressure — "are making contingency plans to strike at the country's adversaries" and that "Iran has assigned different units and organizations to conduct surveillance of opposition figures."[13]

The Wall Street Journal reported that "officials and analysts express concern the incident marks an escalation in Iran's willingness to undertake violent covert operations in the West."[14]

Dignitaries from over 70 countries attended and addressed the Paris Free Iran gathering including many well-known figures from the United States.

Belgian police arrested the two Iranian MOIS agents with a powerful bomb in their possession on June 30, 2018, only hours before the Paris Free Iran gathering.

Two regime agents, Amir Saadouni and Nasimeh Naami, were arrested carrying the explosives. An Iranian diplomat based in Austria, Assadollah Assadi, was the mastermind and according to German federal prosecutors, had personally handed the bomb to the terrorists in Luxembourg.[15] He was subsequently arrested in Germany on July 1. Another individual named Mehrdad Arefani was arrested in France and extradited to Belgium.

According to Belgian police officials, the Albanian police and intelligence services were among those involved in the joint operation to arrest Assadi and foil the terrorist plot.[16] Germany extradited Assadi to Belgium on October 10 to stand trial with his co-conspirators, who are all in prison awaiting judicial processes in Brussels. Reuters reported the diplomat was an Iranian intelligence operative under diplomatic cover.[17]

The Wall Street Journal pointed out that "the plot marked one of the first times that an Iranian official has been caught allegedly taking part in a covert operation in Europe. Police in a number of different European countries are investigating

AGENTEN-KRIMI IM SPESSART!

Plante Iran-Geheimdienstler Anschlag in Paris?

Polizei nahm Assadollah A. an einer deutschen Autobahnraststätte fest

Assadollah Assadi, the mastermind of the terror plot, who personally delivered the bomb to the culprits, was arrested by the German police and is now in jail in Belgium.

alleged attacks against Iranian opposition figures, including two murders in the Netherlands since 2015."[18]

A French diplomatic source told *Agence France Presse* that "the head of operations at the (Iranian) intelligence ministry ordered it."[19]

France froze assets belonging to Tehran's intelligence services and two senior Iranian officials. In a rare joint statement, the French interior, foreign and economy ministers said: "This extremely serious act envisaged on

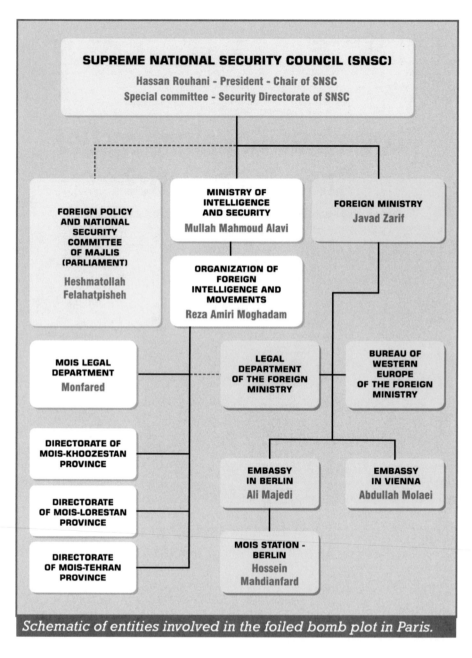

Schematic of entities involved in the foiled bomb plot in Paris.

our territory could not go without a response. ... In taking this decision, France underlines its determination to fight against terrorism in all its forms, particularly on its own territory."[20]

> An Iranian diplomat was the mastermind and had personally handed the bomb to the terrorists in Luxembourg.

Following the French move and announcement by Belgium that Assadi's extradition was complete, U.S. Secretary of State Michael Pompeo issued a statement saying that "The scale of this plot, which involved arrests of numerous suspects across Europe — including in Belgium, France, and Germany — reminds us that Iran remains the world's leading state sponsor of terrorism. This plot also lays bare Iran's continued support of terrorism throughout Europe."[21]

The *New York Times* suggested that "the decision to freeze the assets of the spy ministry seemed to be a clear sign France was angry that Iran appeared to be ignoring international norms and acting with impunity. It also indicated that, at least indirectly, France endorsed Mr. Trump's judgment that Iran was a rogue regime."[22]

U.S. Congress reacts to Paris bombing plot

A House resolution (H.Res 1034 in the 115th Congress), with 105 bi-partisan co-sponsors, was filed in July 2018 in condemnation of "Iranian state-sponsored terrorism and expressing support for the Iranian people's desire for a democratic, secular, and non-nuclear republic of Iran."[23]

Referring to the July 2, 2018 announcement of the Belgium Federal Prosecutor's Office concerning the terrorist bombing plot against the "Free Iran 2018 — the Alternative" gathering in Paris, the resolution condemned "the Iranian regime's terror plot against United States citizens and other participants." The resolution called "on relevant United States Government agencies to work with European allies to identify and bring to justice the Iranian officials behind this plot," and "recognizes the rights of the Iranian people and their struggle to establish a democratic, secular, and non-nuclear republic of Iran."

Separately, Congressman Ted Poe (R-TX), then chairman of Subcommittee on Terrorism, Nonproliferation, and Trade, remarked "We have seen countless times how the mullahs in Iran are not fans of Iranians rallying for freedom. Repeatedly they have responded with violence to crush protests in the streets of Iran, including public hangings of

Iranians from all walks of life participated in the Free Iran gathering in Paris

government protestors. But this year they had the audacity to order an attack on the Iranian dissidents rallying in Paris. European police arrested multiple suspects armed with explosives, including an Iranian diplomat, who intended to target the rally that many Americans, including members of Congress, were attending... Those responsible, including members of the regime in Tehran, must be held accountable."[24]

On July 11, 2018, after Tehran's diplomat, Assadi, was charged by Germany on acting as a foreign agent and conspiracy to commit murder, Secretary Pompeo "accused Iran of using its embassies to plot extremist attacks in Europe," according to the Associated Press.[25]

"Just this past week there were Iranians arrested in Europe who were preparing to conduct a terror plot in Paris, France. We have seen this malign behavior in Europe,"

Secretary Pompeo said in an interview with Sky News Arabia.[26]

The Iran Action Group of the U.S. Department of State in a report entitled "Outlaw Regime: A Chronicle of Iran's Destructive Activities" and released in September 2018, stressed that "Iran uses its MOIS operatives for intelligence collection and clandestine operations outside Iran. As recently as July 2018, an MOIS agent has been implicated in a foiled terror plot on Iranian dissidents in Paris."[27]

NBC News reported on October 4, 2018 that after "the French government officially and publicly blamed Iran's intelligence service for a failed attack on the June gathering of an Iranian opposition group outside Paris attended by thousands, including high-profile Americans like Rudolph Giuliani and Newt Gingrich," U.S. national security adviser John Bolton welcomed France's response, saying, "What the French have done is exactly the right thing. I hope it's a wake-up call across Europe to the nature of the regime and the threat that they pose."[28]

Mayor Rudy Giuliani, Governor Bill Richardson, and Speaker Newt Gingrich were among dozens of senior bi-partisan American dignitaries addressing the Paris rally.

> Tehran is striking out beyond its borders, and has no qualms about conducting a terrorist attack leading to the possible deaths of very high-profile American and European personalities

The same news report quotes a State Department official as saying, "This foiled plot demonstrates that Iran is actively threatening peace and security as the leading state sponsor of terror, not just across the Middle East but globally."[29]

On October 12, 2018, after France pointed a finger at Iran's MOIS for plotting the Paris bomb plot, U.S. Secretary of State Mike Pompeo said that the plan "lays bare Iran's continued support of terrorism throughout Europe," and justifies the re-imposition of sanctions on Tehran."[30]

If there had been any doubt, the events in Paris made it clear that Tehran is striking out beyond its borders, and has no qualms about conducting a terrorist attack leading to the possible deaths of very high-profile American and European personalities, or about the scale of European and American casualties.

Terrorists arrested plotting U.S. operations

The FBI arrested two Iranian citizens, Ahmadreza Mohammadi-Doostdar, 38, and Majid Ghorbani, 59, on August 9. The U.S. Department of Justice, District of Columbia, issued the indictment for the arrests on August 20, alleging that the two residents of California were conducting covert surveillance of Israeli and Jewish facilities in the United States, as well as collecting information about MEK members and other American citizens affiliated with the MEK.[31]

The charges were announced by Assistant Attorney General for National Security John Demers, U.S. Attorney Jessie K. Liu for the District of Columbia and Acting Executive Assistant Director Michael McGarrity of the FBI's National Security Branch.

"Doostdar and Ghorbani are alleged to have acted on behalf of Iran, including by conducting surveillance of political opponents and engaging in other activities that could put Americans at risk," said Assistant Attorney General Demers.[32]

Acting Executive Assistant Director McGarrity added: "This alleged activity demonstrates a continued interest in targeting the United States, as well as potential opposition groups located in the United States."

THE UNITED STATES
DEPARTMENT of JUSTICE

| ABOUT | OUR AGENCY | PRIORITIES | NEWS | RESOURCES | CAREERS |

Home » Office of Public Affairs » News

JUSTICE NEWS

Department of Justice
Office of Public Affairs

FOR IMMEDIATE RELEASE   Monday, August 20, 2018

Two Individuals Charged for Acting as Illegal Agents of the Government of Iran

An indictment was returned today charging Ahmadreza Mohammadi-Doostdar, 38, a dual U.S.-Iranian citizen, and Majid Ghorbani, 59, an Iranian citizen and resident of California, with allegedly acting on behalf of the government of the Islamic Republic of Iran by conducting covert surveillance of Israeli and Jewish facilities in the United States, and collecting identifying information about American citizens and U.S. nationals who are members of the group Mujahedin-e Khalq (MEK).

The charges were announced by Assistant Attorney General for National Security John Demers, U.S. Attorney Jessie K. Liu for the District of Columbia, and Acting Executive Assistant Director Michael McGarrity of the FBI's National Security Branch.

"The National Security Division is committed to protecting the United States from individuals within our country who unlawfully act on behalf of hostile foreign nations," said Assistant Attorney General Demers. "Doostdar and Ghorbani are alleged to have acted on behalf of Iran, including by conducting surveillance of political opponents and engaging in other activities that could put Americans at risk. With their arrest and these charges, we are seeking to hold the defendants accountable."

"This indictment demonstrates the commitment of the Department of Justice to hold accountable agents of foreign governments who act illegally within the United States, especially where those agents are conducting surveillance of individuals and Constitutionally-protected activities in this country," said Jessie K. Liu, United States Attorney for the District of Columbia.

"This alleged activity demonstrates a continued interest in targeting the United States, as well as potential opposition groups located in the United States," said Acting Executive Assistant Director McGarrity. "The FBI will continue to identify and disrupt those individuals who seek to engage in unlawful activity, on behalf of Iran, on US soil."

The indictment charged Doostdar and Ghorbani with knowingly acting as agents of the government of Iran without prior notification to the Attorney General, providing services to Iran in violation of U.S. sanctions, and conspiracy. Both

U.S. Department of Justice announcing the arrest of two Iranian agents in the United States

According to the *Washington Post*, U.S. Magistrate G. Michael Harvey of the District of Columbia, who ordered Ghorbani detained until his trial, said the case as alleged bore "hallmarks of state action," citing the "purported use of code names, counter-surveillance tactics and 'tasking' orders to infiltrate the *Mujahideen-e Khalq* (MEK), or People's Mujahideen of Iran."[33]

Governor Bill Richardson speaking at the May 2018 Iran Freedom Convention, where one of the MOIS agents attended to collect intelligence, according to the Department of Justice.

According to the indictment, "in or about July 2017, Doostdar traveled to the United States from Iran in order to collect intelligence information about entities and individuals considered by the government of Iran to be enemies of that regime, including Israeli and Jewish interests, and individuals associated with the MEK, a group that advocates the overthrow of the current Iranian government."[34]

"This alleged activity demonstrates a continued interest in targeting the United States, as well as potential opposition groups located in the United States."

Doostdar is "alleged to have conducted surveillance of the Rohr Chabad House, a Jewish institution located in Chicago, including photographing the security features surrounding the facility," according to the Department of Justice.[35]

The *Post* reported that "Prosecutors translated Ghorbani's recorded remarks in Farsi as saying he 'penetrated' the MEK to send information back to Tehran for 'targeting' packages."[36]

The criminal complaint and affidavit states that "A human target package includes information collected about an individual, such as the official position of the individual; an analysis of personal vulnerabilities or other opportunities to exploit the individual; and confirmation of the identity and location of the individual. Finally, a target package could enable a neutralization plan, which may include apprehension, recruitment, cyber exploitation, or capture/kill operations."[37]

Court-authorized electronic surveillance revealed Ghorbani telling Doostdar that "he saw the individual who 'leaked the nuclear program'... Jafarzadeh, who is the head of the NCR here — with Safavi..." The Associated Press explained that "one of the people targeted was Alireza Jafarzadeh, deputy director of National Council of Resistance of Iran, Washington office. His revelations about Iran's nuclear sites in 2002 triggered the first inspections in Iran by the International Atomic Energy Agency."[38]

Ghorbani also mentions that he saw Ali Safavi, another NCRI official, during a rally in New York. Ghorbani also mentions that another participant in the rally "needs one — just one shot," apparently referring to a gun shot.[39]

The September 2017 demonstration in front of the United Nations, an event that one of the Iranian regime agents attended to collect intelligence.

According to reports obtained from inside the regime, the MOIS is handling the case with the assistance of the Foreign Ministry. Copies of all reports produced in the Foreign Ministry are submitted to the MOIS office at the Foreign Ministry, which is called the Office for Evaluating Reports. A dossier has been opened on the two detained individuals containing all relevant reports, including the account of the arrests, reports on the indictments, and a letter regarding the identities of the two individuals.

Tehran's spy and terror operations in the United States prompted a swift reaction from U.S. Congress. Senator Marco Rubio (R-Fl), for instance, stated on August 21, 2018 that "We should all be deeply alarmed by @TheJusticeDept's new indictment. Iran's terror-sponsoring regime may be seeking to target American citizens, as well as Jewish or Israeli facilities, on U.S. soil."[40]

Senator Rubio Press ✓
@SenRubioPress

Follow ⌄

We should all be deeply alarmed by @TheJusticeDept's new indictment. Iran's terror-sponsoring regime may be seeking to target American citizens, as well as Jewish or Israeli facilities, on U.S. soil.

> **Two Individuals Charged for Acting as Illegal Agents of the**
> justice.gov
>
> THE UNITED STATES
> DEPARTMENT
> *of* JUSTICE

5:11 PM - 21 Aug 2018

Senator Marco Rubio deeply alarmed about the arrest of two MOIS agents in the U.S.

Assassination plot in Denmark

O n September 28, 2018, much of Denmark came to a halt. A major Danish police operation shut down two key bridges to traffic and halted ferry services to neighboring Sweden and Germany for several hours. The Oresund bridge linking Denmark and Sweden later reopened as hundreds of Danish police and soldiers used cars, sniffer dogs and helicopters to hunt for a black Swedish-registered rental car.[41]

In a press release, the Danish police said that these measures had been taken "in connection with a current

Danish police blocking roads and traffic for hours searching for the would-be assassin

> "An Iranian intelligence agency has planned an assassination on Danish soil. This is completely unacceptable," Denmark's Foreign Minister declared.

investigation" involving the search for "a black Swedish registered Volvo V90" with "probably 3 passengers involved in a serious crime."[42] Asking all witnesses to immediately contact police, the statement ended, "We cannot say more right now, but will get back to you as soon as possible." All transportation links were opened several hours later, although authorities did not provide any more details at the time.[43]

On October 30, Finn Borch Andersen, the head of the Danish Security and Intelligence Service, Politiets Efterretningstjeneste (PET) held a press conference to explain the agency's massive manhunt. The search was part of an attempt to neutralize an assassination plot against a resident of Denmark, he said. "This is a case that entails an Iranian intelligence operation in Denmark. In our view, it was an Iranian intelligence agency's plan to assassinate a person who lives in Denmark."[44]

The PET chief added that the Danish agency had collaborated with Norwegian and Swedish intelligence services, leading to the arrest of a Norwegian-Iranian individual. The arrest occurred in Gothenburg, Sweden, according to the Swedish intelligence service Säpo, and the individual was promptly extradited to Denmark.[45]

Danish Foreign Minister Anders Samuelsen summoned Iran's ambassador, Morteza Moradian, after which the Ministry issued a statement: "As stated by the head of the Danish Security and Service earlier today, the assessment is that an Iranian intelligence agency has planned an assassination on Danish soil. This is completely unacceptable. In fact, the gravity of the matter is difficult to describe. That has been made crystal clear to the Iranian ambassador in Copenhagen today," Denmark's Foreign Minister declared.[46]

Denmark had recalled its ambassador from Tehran and had engaged other EU countries about how to respond. Samuelsen added that Denmark would be in close contact with several like-minded countries regarding the issue of an Iranian intelligence agency's "illegal activities in Europe."[47]

"In light of the latest development, Denmark will now push for a discussion in the EU on the need for further sanctions against Iran," Samuelsen said.[48]

Lars Løkke Rasmussen ✔
@larsloekke

Follow

It is totally unacceptable that Iran or any other foreign state plans assassinations on Danish soil. Further actions against Iran will be discussed in the EU. #dkpol

11:06 AM - 30 Oct 2018

Danish Prime Minister Lars Loekke Rasmussen says further actions against Iran will be discussed in the EU.

The reaction from Washington was swift: "We congratulate the government of Denmark on its arrest of an Iranian regime assassin," U.S. Secretary of State Mike Pompeo said in a tweet. "We call on our allies and partners to confront the full range of Iran's threats to peace and security." [49]

Danish Prime Minister Lars Loekke Rasmussen said in a tweet, "It is totally unacceptable that Iran or any other foreign state plans assassinations on Danish soil. Further actions against Iran will be discussed in the EU."[50]

On November 19, the European Union expressed reaction to the measures taken by France and Denmark. According to Reuters, the foreign ministers of Denmark and France briefed their EU counterparts at a meeting in Brussels on the alleged plots, and the block's ministers "agreed to consider targeted sanctions on Iranians in response."[51]

Information made public by the Iranian Resistance's Security and Counter-terrorism Committee revealed how deeply Tehran was involved with the terror plot and how intensely it had tried to embed its agent in dissident circles, particularly those of the NCRI and MEK. On November 11, the NCRI committee disclosed the name of the Norwegian-Iranian in custody in addition to details about his background and affiliation with Tehran's embassy in Oslo.

Mohammad Davoudzadeh Lului, 39, had been an agent of Iran's Ministry of Intelligence for 10 years. He was arrested on his return from Iran at the Göteborg airport in Sweden on October 21 at the request of the Danish government, and subsequently charged with involvement in a terrorist plot against Iranian-Arab citizens in Denmark.[52]

The NCRI counterterrorism committee also divulged that Davoudzadeh, born in the southwestern city of Ahvaz and a resident of Isfahan in central Iran, was dispatched by the MOIS to Norway in 2008, where he was assigned to pretend to be an asylum seeker in order to eventually acquire Norwegian citizenship. This citizenship was convenient to the missions assigned to him by the MOIS. Despite his legal status as an asylee, Davoudzadeh traveled to Iran many times, an act considered as a betrayal to all refugees and, in accordance with the Geneva Convention and Norwegian laws, one which should have permanently annulled his status.

Throughout the years of his residency in Norway, Davoudzadeh was in close contact with the regime's embassy in Oslo and with its ambassador, Mohammad Hassan Habibollahzadeh. On November 9, the Norwegian media published a photo from a 2018 gathering held at the Iran embassy on the Iranian New Year. Davoudzadeh is seen sitting in the front row next to the regime's ambassador.[53]

Mohammad Davoudzadeh Lului

Per Sandberg, Norway's Minister for Fisheries at that time, and his companion Bahareh Heidari (Letnes), a female Iranian agent of the MOIS, are seated in the front row near Davoudzadeh. Not long after this event, media revelations about Heidari's ties to the MOIS and her attempts to turn Sandberg into an asset forced Sandberg to resign from his post.[54] The MOIS is known for its use of this tactic in luring foreign officials in Norway and elsewhere.[55]

In 2017, the MOIS tasked Davoudzadeh with establishing relations with the offices of the Iranian Resistance in Norway. To this end, he approached MEK supporters in Oslo during anti-regime activities and persistently asked to be put in touch with the Resistance office. Finally, a member of the Iranian Resistance met with him in a cafe in Oslo and noticed significant contradictions in Davoudzadeh's cover story, which made it clear that he was posing as a dissident and most probably was on MOIS assignment.

Further investigation made it almost a certainty that Davoudzadeh was an MOIS agent who had set up several front companies. In February 2018, the issue was discussed, and the information shared, in detail, with Norwegian authorities. In the following months, Davoudzadeh on several occasions contacted MEK supporters on such pretexts as having important intelligence which he intended to share with the MEK. His advances were ignored.

Danish authorities "have obtained a booklet from the Iranian embassy which contains the names of some Iranian exiles who have been referred to as 'terrorists'…"

As mentioned, one of Davoudzadeh's missions in Oslo was to form commercial front companies and front societies, to conduct espionage, to prepare the ground for terrorist acts and to bypass international sanctions. For example, he set up an entity named the Norwegian-Iranian Friendship Association (registration number 919663235) in collaboration with two other individuals, Marjan Gharib (a relative of Davoudzadeh) and Parviz Khodabandeh Shahraki.

Meanwhile, the MOIS set up front companies in the southeastern quake-stricken city of Bam, which required construction and special assistance, through which Davoudzadeh and his front companies could ship banned equipment and goods to Iran. To this end, Davoudzadeh met and coordinated with the manager of Eghtesad Novin Bank in Tehran to discuss the specifics of circumventing the sanctions. In addition, working with the Oslo embassy, particularly its interpreter, Imami, Davoudzadeh facilitated a visit to Norway by the Bam soccer team.

The MOIS was caught off guard when Davoudzadeh was exposed and arrested on October 21, 2018. The agency forced his brother, Mohammad Reza Davoudzadeh, who lived in Isfahan, to guarantee that he and other family members would keep quiet about the arrest in Denmark, and inform the MOIS immediately if anybody referred to it or asked any questions.

On November 3, the state-run daily *Iran*, affiliated with Rouhani's faction, moved to wash the government's hands of the diplomatic debacle. In a commentary entitled "The need for decisive follow up on the Danish issue," the daily wrote: "If there is any connection between the arrested person and Iranian citizens… it is clearly outside national officials' knowledge. If that is the case, decisive action is necessary to root out such rogue actions. Past experience in the chain murders case showed that sometimes there are forces who act arbitrarily and the government and officials have to pay the price…In all such anti-establishment cases, we must uncover the trail of Israeli intelligence in collaboration with the MEK."

The premise contradicts explicit statements on November 5, 2018 by Javad Zarif, the mullahs' foreign minister, who debunked the notion of arbitrary actions in response to a question from a parliament deputy relevant to the secret appendixes of the nuclear deal. "We are not a system which would act arbitrarily… It is not possible to do anything in this country without reporting it."[56]

Meanwhile, the Danish daily newspaper *Jyllands-Posten* wrote that Danish authorities "have obtained a booklet from the Iranian embassy which contains the names of some Iranian exiles who have been referred to as 'terrorists'… Two former heads of the intelligence apparatus believe that this booklet is a kind of terror target list. Danish politicians have asked for an investigation into the Iranian regime's 'hit list.'"[57]

EU nations take action

As its various intelligence and terror operations laid bare the sophisticated web of state-sponsored terror, the Tehran regime found itself facing repercussions for its export of terrorism. In mid-December of 2018, the Albanian government expelled two Iranian diplomats for "damaging national security."[58] The BBC linked the move to the regime's constant threats against the 2,500 MEK members living in Albania.[59]

Not surprisingly, Tehran was defiant in its response. The *Independent* reported that "Iranian officials have described the moves to punish its diplomats as pushed by hardline U.S. officials hostile to the nuclear deal and seeking war with the Islamic Republic."[60]

On January 8, 2019, the European Union voted unanimously to adopt new sanctions against two Iranian individuals and the Iranian Ministry of Intelligence and Security.[61] The sanctioned Iranians are Deputy Minister of Intelligence Saeid Hashemi Moghadam and Assadollah Assadi, currently imprisoned for his role in the Paris terror attack last year.

Denmark's Foreign Minister Anders Samuelsen justified the sanctions, saying "The EU just agreed to enact sanctions against an Iranian Intelligence Service for its assassination plots on European soil. This sends a strong signal from the EU that we will not accept such behavior in Europe."

Additionally, the sanctions targeted the Iranian Ministry of Intelligence and Security. By formally labeling the MOIS as a terrorist entity, the European Union is taking a vital step in targeting the regime's terror apparatus. EU members suggested that further action could be undertaken to punish Iran's involvement in terror attacks.

The regime responded to the sanctions by accusing the EU of supporting the NCRI.[62] The regime's foreign minister, Mohammad Javad Zarif, cited the significant presence of NCRI members in European states as evidence, reflecting the mullahs' fear that the parliament-in-exile is gaining internal and international support aimed at toppling the regime.

The actions taken by the Albanian government and EU signal a shift after years of international disregard of the clerical regime's extensive terror activities. European intelligence services are well aware that they must continue to be watchful, as the desperate regime becomes ever more reckless in its attacks.

Chapter Two

Tehran's Embassies: HQs for Terrorism

T he theocratic system that came to power in Iran in 1979 lacked the historical, political, and social capacity to meet the needs of the Iranian society. It has consequently maintained its hold on power by two means: internal repression and the spread of extremism and terrorism abroad.

In the early years, Tehran infamously masterminded numerous hijackings and bombings, such as that of the U.S. Marine barracks in Beirut, Lebanon, on October 23, 1983. Iranian regime's then Minister of the Islamic Revolutionary Guards Corps (IRGC), Mohsen Rafiqdoust, bragged to the media that "both the TNT and the ideology which in one blast sent to hell 400 officers, NCOs, and soldiers at the Marine Headquarters were provided by Iran." [63]

Terrorism had been on the agenda since the regime's inception, but after its failure in the war with Iraq in 1988, Tehran infused terror as a foreign policy tactic into the governmental system. One French official who investigated Iranian state-sponsored terrorism said in 1994, "The whole Iranian state apparatus is at the service of these operations."[64] It was institutionalized as a tool of statecraft and made the responsibility of certain institutions. Domestic terror served as a tool for repressing dissent and continuing the regime's rule. Abroad, terrorism became a means of dictating and promoting Tehran's foreign policy.

Several European court cases and judicial decisions have confirmed that all the regime's terrorist acts are ordered at the highest levels, specifically the Supreme National Security Council, which is the top decision-maker in the defense/security apparatus and is headed by the president,

۲۹ /تیر/ ۷۰

سخنرانی برادر محسن رفیق دوست در یکی از کارخانجات صنایع دفاع کشور

در پیروزی انقلاب در لبنان و در خیلی از جاهای دنیا، آمریکا ضرب شست ما را بر پیکر منحوس خودش احساس می کند و می داند آن مواد منفجره ای که با آن ایدئولوژی ترکیب شد و در مقرّ تفنگدارهای دریایی چهارصد افسر و درجه دار و سرباز را یک مرتبه به جهنم فرستاد. هم تی ان تی آن مال ایران بود و هم ایدئولوژیش از ایران رفته بود. این برای آمریکا بسیار محسوس است، فلذاست که در خلیج فارس درمانده شده.

State-run Ressalat newspaper, July 20, 1987, Mohsen Rafiqdoust, minister of the Revolutionary Guards Corps: "Both the TNT and the ideology which in one blast sent to hell 400 officers, NCO's, and soldiers at the Marine Headquarters were provided by Iran."

Hassan Rouhani. The regime's Supreme Leader, Ali Khamenei, ultimately approves all such orders.[65]

Embassies provide the safe haven for the intelligence apparatus and its terrorists, and thus play a special role in organizing, facilitating and executing terrorist operations.[66] This is especially true of Tehran's embassies in Europe, but also applies to diplomatic facilities, interest sections, and "diplomats" elsewhere. The "Iranian connection" to Islamic fundamentalist terrorism has been described as "a worldwide network of embassies and diplomatic missions — staffed with intelligence personnel — which shelters terrorists, stores their weaponry, and monitors potential targets."[67]

Tehran's Ministry of Intelligence and Security (MOIS) has systematically set up its intelligence stations within the embassies to exploit diplomatic immunity and passports for

The "Iranian connection" to Islamic fundamentalist terrorism has been described as "a worldwide network of embassies and diplomatic missions — staffed with intelligence personnel — which shelters terrorists, stores their weaponry, and monitors potential targets."

its terrorists, as well as diplomatic pouches for the transfer of weapons, equipment and cash. MOIS agents, and more recently the Quds Force, run operations out of Iranian embassies, consulates, and Islamic cultural centers overseas. Using diplomatic cover and immunity, they command terrorist operations, and provide intelligence, logistics, and cash.[68]

The 1980s and early 1990s saw a dozen Iranian terrorist operations in European countries, including the assassinations of several prominent opposition figures. The most well-known was Professor Kazem Rajavi who, on April 24, 1990, was gunned down in broad daylight by several agents of the Ministry of Intelligence and Security as he was driving to his home in Coppet, a village near Geneva.

Professor Kazem Rajavi at the United Nations where he was first post-revolution ambassador in Geneva.

Rajavi's assassination required enormous resources, considerable planning, and coordination among several of the regime's organizations. After extensive investigations, Roland Chatelain, the Swiss magistrate in charge of the case, and Swiss judicial and police officials confirmed the role of Iran's government and the participation of thirteen official agents of Tehran who had used "service passports"

> MOIS agents, and more recently the Quds Force, run operations out of Iranian embassies, consulates, and Islamic cultural centers overseas.

issued by Iran's Foreign Ministry to enter Switzerland for their plot.

The Mykonos trial in 1997 marked a turning point in the methodology of Tehran's murderers. The Mykonos Tribunal in Germany condemned the assassination of four leaders

Assassins sent from Tehran attacked Professor Rajavi and killed him as he was driving to his home in Geneva.

Four leaders of Kurdish opposition groups were murdered by the hit squad directed by Iran's embassy in Germany, at the Mykonos Restaurant in Berlin in 1992. The assassination was authorized by the regime's Supreme Leader Ali Khamenei.

of Kurdish opposition groups at the Mykonos Restaurant in Berlin in 1992. The regime's top leadership — including both the Supreme Leader and president — and its diplomatic missions were directly tied to the terror operation targeting the dissidents. "On September 17, 1992, when a hit squad, upon the orders of the Iranian statesmen murdered the leaders of the Kurdish opposition (Democratic Party of Iranian Kurdistan), in Mykonos Restaurant in Berlin, from a judicial perspective, Europe had turned into a so-called free zone for murderers with diplomatic passports."[69]

Afterwards, Iranian operatives created dormant cells and kept intelligence stations in the regime's embassies, continued their spying activity against the opposition and Western countries, and remained on standby to carry out

> "On September 17, 1992, when a hit squad, murdered the leaders of the Kurdish opposition, in Mykonos Restaurant in Berlin, from a judicial perspective, Europe had turned into a so-called free zone for murderers with diplomatic passports."

their terror plots when and where necessary. The annual reports from the German and Dutch intelligence services after 1997 show the continuity of these activities.

In the wake of this change, terrorist activities and operations continued and expanded in the Middle East region and particularly in Iraq. From around 2008, the regime launched terrorist activities in Asian and African countries, including in Turkey, Georgia, India, Malaysia, Thailand and Kenya. The regime's terrorist operations in Europe and the United States resumed in 2011, when on October 11, the Prosecutor for the District of Southern New York filed charges against an Iranian-American, Mansoor Arbabsiar, and a senior commander of the IRGC Quds Force, Ali Gholam Shakuri for orchestrating an elaborate murder-for-hire plot. According to the plot, Arbabsiar, under the command of Shakuri, was to pay 1.5 million dollars to drug dealers to kill Adel al-Jubeir, the Saudi envoy to Washington at the time, by blowing up a restaurant in the middle of Washington, D.C. (Mr. Jubeir later became the Saudi Minister of Foreign Affairs and is currently the Minister of State for Foreign Affairs).[70] Arbabsiar pleaded guilty and was sentenced to 25 years imprisonment.[71]

Iranian terror attacks have recently entered a new phase in Europe with an upward trend. This uptick can be explained in the context of three important developments which have taken place since the second half of 2016. First, several thousand members of the People's Mojahedin Organization of Iran were transferred from Iraq to Albania. The regime had intended to massacre all of them in Iraq, making their safe transfer to Europe a strategic failure for Tehran. Second, economic and social crises, coupled with profound social dissatisfaction erupted into nationwide anti-government protests that began in late 2017 and have continued throughout 2018 and 2019. And third, the previous U.S. administrations' conciliatory policy toward the regime had greatly contributed to its survival. Recent changes in that policy, including the U.S. withdrawal from the Joint Comprehensive Plan of Action (JCPOA), also

> Terrorism has always been a tool of statecraft for the mullahs, but now it has taken on new dimensions, particularly in Europe, as the regime struggles to survive.

> The June 2018 terrorist plot targeting the gathering in Paris demonstrates that Tehran's terrorism poses a threat not only to the Iranian opposition and Iranian refugees, but also to the security of Europe and its people. It is a threat which the West ignores to its detriment.

known as the nuclear deal, have drastically affected the regime's political outlook.

These changes have shaken the regime to its core. Terrorism has always been a tool of statecraft for the mullahs, but now it has taken on new dimensions, particularly in Europe, as the regime struggles to survive. The MOIS has established more facilities for foreign terrorism, and the regime's top-level terrorist activities are being planned and coordinated at key embassies and information stations in Europe. Embassies are in fact safe havens for espionage, logistics and terrorist operations.

The June 2018 terrorist plot targeting the gathering in Paris demonstrates that Tehran's terrorism poses a threat not only to the Iranian opposition and Iranian refugees, but also to the security of Europe and its people. It is a threat which the West ignores to its detriment.

Albania

A small country with few, if any, ties to Iran, Albania has a long tradition of standing firm against extremism and intolerance, demonstrating its cultural civility as the only country in Europe where the Jewish population experienced growth during the Holocaust.

When MEK members living in Iraq reached out in the aftermath of rocket attacks and a massacre at the hands of the regime's agents in May 2013, the government of Albania began accepting them as refugees. That same year, the regime's Ministry of Intelligence and Security (MOIS) began sending intelligence agents to its embassy in Tirana, which had never had more than two or three diplomats, whether

Iran's embassy in Tirana, Albania

during the era of the shah or the rule of the clerics. Since the MEK has taken up residence in Albania, the mullahs' embassy in Tirana has become one of the most important Iranian embassies in Europe.

MOIS agent Fereydoun Zandi Ali Abadi headed up the first intelligence station in Tirana from early 2014 to 2017. His primary mission was gathering intelligence on the MEK and identifying their whereabouts in Albania.

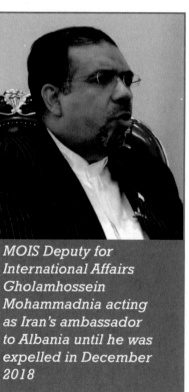

MOIS Deputy for International Affairs Gholamhossein Mohammadnia acting as Iran's ambassador to Albania until he was expelled in December 2018

In 2016, MOIS Deputy for International Affairs Gholamhossein Mohammadnia became the regime's ambassador in Albania, and the embassy increasingly came under the control of MOIS agents.

In 2017, Mostafa Roudaki, who had been in charge of the intelligence station in the regime's embassy in Austria and at one time oversaw all of the MOIS operations in Europe, became the head of station in Albania, and was tasked with stepping up the espionage and terrorist activities against the MEK in the wake of the uprisings in Iran.

One such terror attack on the facility housing more than 2,500 MEK members was plotted for the eve of the Iranian New Year celebration (*Nowruz*) in March 2018. As discussed in Chapter 1, the terrorists planned to use a truck bomb to blow up the large *Nowruz* gathering attended by Resistance leaders, including NCRI President-elect Maryam Rajavi, and VIPs from the U.S. and Europe. The plot was foiled by the security services of Albania, who arrested two regime agents who had entered Albania under the guise of reporters.

Roudaki has also hired MEK defectors who act as foot soldiers in carrying out the MOIS conspiracies and are paid to slander and disseminate false information against the Iranian Resistance and the MEK.

The regime's embassy in Albania recruits MEK defectors for espionage and information about the MEK's residences and headquarters, which it then uses in planning terrorist attacks against the group. Some of the more well-known agents of MOIS have traveled to Albania from other European countries for this purpose.

One of the agents recruited by the regime's embassy to form intelligence networks in Tirana is Ehsan Bidi,

Roudaki has also hired MEK defectors who act as foot soldiers in carrying out the MOIS conspiracies and are paid to slander and disseminate false information against the Iranian Resistance and the MEK.

who coordinates the regime's intelligence recruits at the embassy. Bidi receives cash payments from the embassy and subsequently doles out money to the other intelligence operatives.

Ehsan Bidi entered Albania on 16 October 2013 as a refugee and 'former MEK member' on an Iranian passport issued by the MOIS. That passport, registered on 27 January 2013, and valid for five years, numbered 16359072. Therefore, there is no justification for recognizing this individual as a refugee, as the representatives of the MEK voiced their protest to the UN High Commissioner for Refugees in 2013.[72]

Two other intelligence agents in contact with Bidi travel to Albania from Britain. Massoud Khodabandeh and his wife Anne Khodabandeh (Singleton) are assigned to conduct media and TV interviews with individuals recruited by the MOIS to spread misinformation and lies against the MEK. The individuals involved are paid for their roles in these vilification campaigns. According to a Library of Congress report, Khodabandeh and Singleton have both been working for the MOIS for years.[73]

Working with the regime's Ministry of Foreign Affairs, the MOIS has also brought two of its off-shoots, the Habilian Center and the Dideban Institute, to Albania. Under the false pretexts of cultural and press activities, the two entities reinforce Roudaki's anti-MEK intel and PR activities.

Many MOIS schemes are conducted under the cover of cultural activities in Tirana and, more recently, even in Tehran. For example, a meeting was held on March 5 and 6, 2018, in Tehran, supposedly to commemorate major supporters of the group. MEK has made numerous terrorist attacks on Iranian interests inside and outside of Iran. The Iranian government and its intelligence apparatus consider MEK the most serious dissident organization with regard to the Revolution.

MEK's main base is Camp Ashraf in Iraq. With the fall of the Ba'ath regime in Iraq in 2003, the group lost this major support. After the 1991 Persian Gulf War against Iraq, MOIS made anti-MEK psychological warfare one of its main objectives, but MEK nonetheless has remained a viable organization. Aside from MEK, MOIS assassins also targeted opposition figures in cities abroad such as Baghdad, Berlin, Dubai, Geneva, Istanbul, Karachi, Oslo, Paris, Rome, and Stockholm.[61]

The recruitment of a British subject, Anne Singleton, and her Iranian husband, Masoud Khodabandeh, provides a relevant example of how MOIS coerces non-Iranians to cooperate. She worked with MEK in the late 1980s. Masoud Khodabandeh and his brother Ibrahim were both members of MEK at the time. In 1996 Masoud Khodabandeh decided to leave the organization. Later, he married Anne Singleton. Soon after their

Anne Singleton and Masoud Khodabandeh
Source: http://www.mesconsult.com/

marriage, MOIS forced them to cooperate by threatening to confiscate Khodabandeh's mother's extensive property in Tehran. Singleton and Khodabandeh then agreed to work for MOIS and spy on MEK. In 2002 Singleton met in Tehran with MOIS agents who were interested in her background. She agreed to cooperate with MOIS to save her brother-in-law's life—he was still a member of MEK at the time. During her stay in Tehran, she received training from MOIS. After her return to England, she launched the *iran-interlink.org* Web site in the winter of 2002. After she made many trips to Iran and Singapore—the country where the agency contacts its foreign agents—MEK became doubtful of Singleton and Khodabandeh's loyalty to the organization. In 2004 Singleton finally met her brother-in-law, Ibrahim, who was sent from Syria to Iran after the

[61] "Masters of Disinformation," *Iran Terror Database*, November 22, 2005, 2, http://www.iranterror.com/index2.php?option=com_content&do_pdf=1&id=113 (accessed April 11, 2012); "Mujahedeen-e Khalq (MEK)," Federation of American Scientists, Intelligence Resource Program, July 13, 2004, http://www.fas.org/irp/world/para/mek.htm (accessed May 18, 2012).

According to a Library of Congress report, Massoud Khodabandeh and Anne Khodabandeh (Singleton) have both been working for the MOIS for years

the 19th century Albanian poet Naim Frashëri. The MOIS and embassy in Tirana brought a number of Albanian and Balkan nationals to Tehran, where MOIS agents such as Ebrahim Khodabandeh, a representative of the MOIS-run

> Working with the regime's Ministry of Foreign Affairs, the MOIS has also brought two of its off-shoots, the Habilian Center and the Dideban Institute, to Albania.

Nejat Association, were on hand to speak with them and spread anti-MEK propaganda.

Recruited by the MOIS back in 2003, Ebrahim Khodabandeh traveled frequently to Iraq to encourage Iraqi mercenaries to exert pressure on the MEK in Iraq. Anne Khodabandeh (Singleton), another MOIS agent and Ebrahim Khodabandeh's sister-in-law, was dispatched to Albania three times in November 2017 to take part in MOIS conspiracies against the MEK.

On December 19, 2018, Albania's Foreign Ministry announced that Iran's Ambassador, Mohammadnia, and Roudaki, the head of station, had both been expelled for their roles in the plot to bomb the MEK gathering. Despite the expulsion of two of its intelligence agents, Tehran continues its intelligence activities under the direction of another intelligence operative named Mohammad Ali Hossein Arzpeima Nemati, who also resides at the embassy.

Austria

For several years, the embassy in Vienna, Austria has served as the MOIS hub in Europe. The Vienna embassy played a central role in Tehran's latest and potentially most deadly terror plot in Europe, to bomb the annual Iran Freedom rally in Paris on June 30, 2018. The conference was attended by tens of thousands of MEK and NCRI supporters and hundreds of American and European dignitaries.

The plot was foiled by European intelligence services. On June 30, the Belgian Federal Police arrested a Belgian-Iranian couple in the suburbs of Brussels with 500 grams of TATP explosive. A detonator was found hidden in the woman's toiletries bag.

Iran's embassy in Vienna, Austria

The gas station where Asadollah Assadi was apprehended by German authorities after he personally delivered a bomb to the would-be bombers in Luxemburg - DPA

On July 1, German authorities arrested the Iranian diplomat in charge of the operation, Asadollah Assadi, head of the intelligence station at the Vienna embassy. Assadi had been stationed there under the title of Third Consular since June 3, 2014. According to a German Federal Prosecutor's notice, Assadi personally delivered the bomb to the would-be bombers in Luxemburg.[74]

The extensive presence of MOIS agents in Austria is well-known. An Austrian newspaper, *Die Presse*, reported on January 8, 2013 that Vienna was "full of spies for the Islamic Republic. Some are Iranian, and some are citizens of other countries." The Federal Research Division of the U.S. Congress in 2012 reported Tehran had about 100 spies in Austria.[75]

The embassy in Vienna provided logistics for the 1989 assassination of the Secretary-General of the Kurdistan Democratic Party of Iran, Abdul Rahman Ghassemlou on

The embassy in Vienna provided logistics for the 1989 assassination of the Secretary-General of the Kurdistan Democratic Party of Iran, Abdul Rahman Ghassemlou, and two other Kurds.

July 13, 1989, by the IRGC's intelligence section and its Ramadan Garrison, which later became the Quds Force.[76] Ghassemlou was killed along with two other Kurds during negotiations with the mullahs' regime in Vienna.

The commander of Ramadan Garrison, Mohammad Jafari Sahraroudi, alias Rahimi Sahraroudi, the IRGC's intelligence commander for exterritorial operations, had gone to Vienna ostensibly for talks with DPIK officials. He was in fact the commander of the hit squad who were reportedly brought to the meeting place and site of the assassination in an embassy car.

Sahraroudi was hit by a stray bullet from another gunman during the attack. He was arrested by police and hospitalized.[77] Peter Pilz, a former member of the Austrian

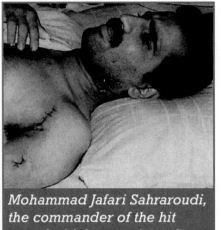

Mohammad Jafari Sahraroudi, the commander of the hit squad which assassinated Abdul Rahman Ghassemlou in Vienna, was hit by a stray bullet from another gunman during the attack. Days later, he was flown back to Iran.

Parliament, detailed his extensive investigation of the assassination in his book *Escort to Tehran*, noting how the assassins were able to escape justice due to the intervention of the regime in general and its Embassy in Vienna specifically. Sahraroudi was taken to the airport under police escort on July 22, 1989 and returned to Tehran on Iran Air flight number IR722.[78] Five members of the Iranian embassy escorted him to the airport.[79]

In his memoirs, Ali Akbar Hashemi Rafsanjani, one of the regime's most senior officials from its inception and its president at the time of Ghassemlou's assassination, wrote in detail how he had personally pursued the case of Sahraroudi until he was returned to Iran.

Amir Mansour Bozorgian, another member of the hit squad, was also arrested after the attack, but was released on the morning of July 15, 1989. He went directly to the regime's Vienna embassy, where he took refuge for several months before eventually fleeing to Iran. The Austrian judiciary issued an international arrest warrant for Sahraroudi and Bozorgian in November of that year.[80]

France

The regime's embassy in France is one of the most active and critical nodes in its terror network in Europe. Throughout the 1980s, it primarily targeted the headquarters of the opposition coalition, the National Council of Resistance of Iran (NCRI). MOIS intelligence officers including Gholam Hossein Mesbah and Hamid Reza Abotalebi called the shots.

After the role of the embassy in Germany was exposed during the trial of the Mykonos assassins, the mullahs decided to take a more cautious approach in Germany and

Iran's embassy in France

Ali Vakili Rad who assassinated Shapur Bakhtiar in Paris in 1991, was returned to Iran in 2010, where the regime gave him a hero's welcome.

instead accelerate their activities in France. As a result, the mission and role of the Paris embassy expanded in every sense, including espionage, intelligence, and export of fundamentalism and terrorism.

Hamid Ebadi, aka Ahmad Zarif, the head of the Intelligence station at the regime's embassy in Paris, is tasked with coordinating the activities targeting Iranian Resistance activists and refugees in France. In recent years, this has involved espionage, disturbances, and other measures against the annual Resistance gatherings in Paris. In August 2015, the embassy intelligence unit dispatched two notorious agents, Ghorban Ali Hossein Nejad and Mostafa Mohammadi, to engage in terrorist acts in the vicinity of the NCRI's office, but they were arrested by Gendarmerie and expelled from the area.

On August 6, 1991, Shapur Bakhtiar, the Shah's last prime minister, was killed along with his assistant by three assassins in Paris.[81] One of the assassins was an MOIS agent, who had infiltrated Bakhtiar's inner circle and worked as an assistant in his office.[82] After the assassination, one terrorist named Ali Vakili Rad, who had been dispatched from Iran, escaped to Switzerland. Zeinalabedin Sarhaddi, who was serving at the regime's embassy in Switzerland as a diplomat, was arrested for his role in the assassination. Switzerland handed both over to France, where they were prosecuted and imprisoned. In 2010, however, before either had served his full sentence, French authorities released both men amid talk about a "deal" with Tehran and sent them to Iran, where Vakili Rad received a hero's welcome.[83]

Massoud Hendi another culprit in Bakhtiar's 1991 assassination.

Massoud Hendi was another culprit in Bakhtiar's case. A relative of Ruhollah Khomeini, he worked as the head of the office of Iran Radio & Television at the embassy in Paris. He was sentenced to 10 years in prison.[84]

Germany

Prior to the Mykonos verdict in 1997, all MOIS espionage and terrorist activities in Europe were coordinated from the regime's embassy in Germany. At the time situated in Bonn, it was the MOIS hub in the heart of Europe.

According to German prosecutors, three arms of Iran's secret services operate in Germany: the Ministry of Intelligence and Security, the IRGC's Quds Force, and the Iranian army's counterespionage branch. Each has separate objectives, but cooperate with each other in organizing covert operations under the cover of straw companies. All three maintain representatives in Germany, whose official offices are in the Iranian Embassy in Bonn. The MOIS

Iran's embassy in Germany

> According to German prosecutors, three arms of Iran's secret services operate in Germany: the Ministry of Intelligence and Security, the IRGC's Quds Force, and the Iranian army's counterespionage branch.

office had been set up in 1986 on the third floor of the embassy.[85]

The German Federal Office for the Protection of the Constitution reported that the main mission of the regime's embassy in Germany is espionage activities against the opposition forces, in particular the NCRI and MEK. The annual report published in 1999 said the MEK and NCRI are "at the heart of Iran's intelligence service plots."[86]

The latest report (2017) of the Office for the Protection of the Constitution in North Rhine-Westphalia says: "In North Rhine-Westphalia as in the whole of Germany, the intelligence activities of Iran are mainly from the Ministry of Information and Security (MOIS). The MOIS is the civilian domestic and foreign intelligence service of the Islamic Republic of Iran. MOIS observes mainly opposition forces operating in exile, in particular the People's Mojahedin Organization of Iran (MEK), and its political arm, the National Council of Resistance of Iran (NCRI) strongly represented in North Rhine-Westphalia. The MOIS

> MOIS observes mainly opposition forces operating in exile, in particular the People's Mojahedin Organization of Iran (MEK)

tries to monitor the exile opposition by infiltration and to discredit it with targeted propaganda."[87]

Among several high-profile assassinations in Germany, the Mykonos murders are perhaps the most notorious. On September 18, 1992, the Secretary General of the Democratic Party of Iranian Kurdistan, Sadegh Sharafkandi, was assassinated with three members of his team at the Mykonos Restaurant in Berlin. According to a report from the German Intelligence Agency, the murders were planned and implemented under the leadership of Iranian diplomatic missions. The operation's codename, discovered by the BFV after the attack and confirmed by witnesses, was *"faryad-e bozorg-e alavi."* According to reports obtained by the Berlin courts from the police, as well as evidence of recorded phone calls during the terrorist operations, the codename had been announced by the regime's embassy in Germany. The entire operation was carried out through the Iranian embassy in Bonn.

The trial began in October 1993 and lasted nearly three and a half years. A total of 176 witnesses were called, and the documents presented ran to 187 binders.[88] The federal court of Berlin announced on April 10, 1997 that

Mullah Ali Fallahian, regime Minister of Intelligence and Security (1989 to 1997), implicated by German courts for his role in the 1992 Mykonos murders.

the highest authorities in Tehran had issued the decree ordering the assassination.[89] Kazem Darabi, the mastermind of this assassination, who was arrested and sentenced to life imprisonment, had direct connections with the Iranian embassy in Bonn. Following the Mykonos Court verdict, all European countries recalled their ambassadors from Iran for several weeks. During the trial, German prosecutor Bruno Jost issued an arrest warrant for Ali Fallahian, the regime's Minister of Intelligence at the time.[90]

Another assassination, this time averted, was reported on June 25, 1995. The *New York Times* quoted American security officials as saying that Iranian diplomats based at the Iranian embassy in Bonn had a plan to assassinate Mrs.

> The federal court of Berlin announced on April 10, 1997 that the highest authorities in Tehran had issued the decree ordering the assassination.

U.S. Asserts Iranians Plotted To Disrupt Rally in Germany

By ELAINE SCIOLINO

WASHINGTON, June 24 — Iranian diplomats working out of their embassy in Bonn plotted to disrupt a huge opposition rally in Germany last week, perhaps with the intention of assassinating a leading Iranian dissident, American intelligence officials said today.

At about the same time, Germany asked two Iranian intelligence officials to leave the country because of evidence that they were planning potentially lethal operations from German territory, the American officials said. The expulsions did not appear to be specifically linked to the plot.

German Foreign Ministry officials denied any knowledge of the plot or the expulsions, although they abruptly banned the opposition leader, Maryam Rajavi, from entering the country to address the rally.

But United States officials said they confirmed the incidents both with German officials and through independent American intelligence-gathering efforts in Germany.

The American disclosure of the incident in Bonn is likely to embarrass the German Government and may further divide the Clinton Ad-

Since Germany has led the Europeans in defending what it calls a "critical dialogue" with Teheran that is based on high-level exchanges and efforts to boost trade, it is not surprising that German authorities have kept quiet about the alleged plot, but have clung to the official line.

"We cannot allow cause for the violent overthrow of a government from our own territory," said Sabine Sparwasser, a Foreign Ministry spokesman in Bonn. Asked whether Germany has asked for the expulsion of two Iranian diplomats, she added, "To my knowledge there have been no recent cases where we told Iranians from the embassy to leave."

Officials in the office of Bernd Schmidbauer, the intelligence coordinator for Chancellor Helmut Kohl and the senior German official involved in contacts with Iran, declined comment on any matter involving Iran. It was Mr. Schmidbauer who infuriated the Clinton Administration after he allowed Ali Fallahian, the head of Iran's intelligence services, to visit Germany in 1993, and tour intelligence headquarters in Wiesbaden.

New York Times quotes American security officials as saying that Iranian diplomats based at the Iranian embassy in Bonn planned to assassinate Mrs. Maryam Rajavi at a gathering of Iranians in Dortmund, Germany, in 1995.

Maryam Rajavi at a gathering of Iranians in Dortmund, Germany. U.S. officials said that Germany had expelled two Iranian intelligence agents due to evidence that they were designing operations that could have been fatal.[91] The NCRI identified the two terrorist diplomats as Ali Osuli and Jalal Abbasi.

> The New York Times quoted American security officials as saying that Iranian diplomats based at the Iranian embassy in Bonn had a plan to assassinate Mrs. Maryam Rajavi at a gathering of Iranians in Dortmund, Germany.

Osuli later contacted the Ministry of Intelligence in Tehran, telling them that the Dortmund plot was "a very calculated plan, and things were going very well, perfectly, but because of a problem with one of the services, the plan was ruined." He added: "If the foreigners had not been foolish, the story in Dortmund would have been recorded in history."[92]

According to the *New York Times*, U.S. and German intelligence agencies concluded that Iran used its embassy in Bonn as "an informal headquarters" for its intelligence services in Europe and the purchase of military equipment. The embassy was also used as a base for monitoring 100,000 Iranian citizens in Germany.[93]

The German prosecutor announced on April 8, 2016, that Meysam Panahi, 31, had been arrested for spying on the MEK on behalf of the MOIS.[94] Panahi had received payments from a senior MOIS official on at least 30

> According to the New York Times, U.S. and German intelligence agencies concluded that Iran used its embassy in Bonn as "an informal headquarters" for its intelligence services in Europe.

occasions. He was sentenced to 2 years and 4 months imprisonment on July 19, 2016.

On July 7, 2016, the Office of the German prosecutor's office announced the arrest of a 31-year-old Pakistani national named Syed Mustufa Haydar in the city of Bremen on charges of spying for Iran. Federal prosecutors said that he was "in contact with an intelligence unit attributed to Iran." He was charged with spying on Reinhold Robbe, the former lawmaker and former head of the German-Israeli Society, and a French-Israeli professor in Frankfort, in October 2015.[95] The prosecutors told the court that Haydar was being directed by someone from the Quds Force.[96] He was sentenced to four years and three months in prison.[97]

German Special Forces acting on the order of the country's Federal Prosecutor raided 10 targets allegedly belonging to agents affiliated to the Quds Force in the states of Baden-Wurttemberg, North Rhine-Westphalia, Bavaria and Berlin on January 16, 2018.[98]

Italy

On March 16, 1993, Mohammad Hossein Naghdi, Representative of the National Council of Resistance of Iran in Italy, was assassinated by Iranian terrorists. Mr. Naghdi was a former Iranian diplomat who had worked at Tehran's Rome embassy. In 1982, angered by the suppression of dissidents after the revolution, he defected to the opposition.[99]

The agent sent from Tehran to kill Mr. Naghdi was supervised and controlled in Italy by Tehran's ambassador, Hamid Abutalebi.[100] In addition to being ambassador to Italy from 1987 to 1991, Abutalebi had been ambassador

Iran's embassy in Italy.

Mohammad Hossein Naghdi, Representative of the National Council of Resistance of Iran in Italy, was assassinated by Iranian terrorists on March 16, 1993.

in Australia, Belgium and the European Union.[101] In 2013, Abutalebi was appointed as the political deputy of the office of President Rouhani.[102]

In 2014, the regime decided to send Abutalebi as its ambassador to the United Nations. The U.S. House of Representatives unanimously passed legislation to bar him from entering the United States for having "engaged in terrorist activity against the United States,"[103] and the U.S. government refused to grant him a visa because of his part in the U.S. Embassy siege in Tehran in 1979 and his participation in Naghdi's assassination.[104]

The agent sent from Tehran to kill Mr. Naghdi was supervised and controlled in Italy by Iran's's ambassador, Hamid Abutalebi.

Mr Naghdi was shot on a Rome street in a murder that has never been solved. Investigations continued into the case until 2008, when the Rome Appeals Court published evidence that the Iranian state had ordered his death. The British newspaper *Daily Telegraph* wrote on April 9, 2014: "Court papers, including transcripts of interviews conducted by the *Carabinieri* during the investigation into Naghdi's death, allege that [Amir Mansur Assl Bozorgian, the head of Iranian intelligence in Rome] played a key role in covert operations in the 1990s.[105]

According to the summary judgment issued on Dec 16, 2008, "The execution was planned by high ranking political-religious officials in Tehran, with the task entrusted to a group sent specially to Italy, coordinated there by the accused, Bozorgian, in his role as head of a logistics and information unit... directly answerable to the Iranian

The Rome Criminal Court ruled that decision to kill [Naghdi] was taken by a group of Tehran's political and religious leaders and assigned to the group led by Bozorgian, ... in full coordination with the Iranian embassy in [Italy] and in particular with Ambassador Abutalebi."

diplomatic representative in our country, in particular the ambassador Abutalebi."

It added that Abutalebi and Naghdi had a previous acquaintance and that the ambassador was in the country at the time of his death.[106]

The Rome Criminal Court ruled that "Naghdi's murder should be considered as a political murder, which has been decided in the Iranian government's circles in the framework of a larger project aimed at destroying resistance centers abroad. Due to his political activity in Italy, due to his ability to establish a relationship with the highest levels of political circle in Italy, due to the undeniable human abilities, and for the ... unceasing struggle with a clear and obvious face against the regime which he initially had embraced. The decision to kill [Naghdi] was taken by a group of Tehran's political and religious leaders and assigned to the group led by Bozorgian, ... in full coordination with the Iranian embassy in [Italy] and in particular with Ambassador Abutalebi."[107]

Sweden

In late 1993, the mullahs plotted the assassinations of some Iranian Resistance officials planning a trip to Sweden. The MOIS plan was for two agents, Jamshid Abedi and Simin Ghorbani, to infiltrate the MEK. The MOIS plot was foiled, the two agents arrested, and three diplomats from the regime's embassy expelled on November 15, 1993. The regime retaliated by expelling a Swedish diplomat from Tehran on November 17, 1993 and reducing economic ties with Sweden.[108]

In 2008, the Swedish government expelled Hassan Saleh Majd, a diplomat terrorist, as *persona non grata*. According to the Swedish Security Police, "an intelligence officer was expelled from Sweden. The individual worked at his country's embassy in Stockholm. However, instead of performing diplomatic activities as an embassy advisor, he systematically worked against people from his country who had taken refuge in Sweden."[109] In retaliation, Tehran expelled a Swedish diplomat in late February 2008.[110]

Switzerland

Iran's embassy in Bern, as well as its UN representative office in Geneva, have been used extensively to provide diplomatic cover for agents of the various intelligence units of MOIS.

On April 24, 1990, terrorists assassinated Professor Kazem Rajavi, Iran's first Ambassador to the United Nations headquarters in Geneva following the 1979 Revolution. Shortly after his appointment, Rajavi resigned his post in protest to the "repressive policies and terrorist activities of the ruling clerics in Iran," and intensified his campaign against the mass executions,

Iran's embassy in Switzerland.

arbitrary arrests, and torture carried out by Iran's theocratic leadership.

Dr. Rajavi became the NCRI representative in Switzerland, where he was a Geneva University professor. He was gunned down on the way to his home in the outskirts of Geneva. Sirous Nasseri, the regime's ambassador to the United Nations, had publicly threatened in February 1990 to "eliminate" Kazem Rajavi.[111] The Iranian Resistance

On April 24, 1990, terrorists dispatched from Tehran assassinated Professor Kazem Rajavi, Iran's first Ambassador to the United Nations headquarters in Geneva following the 1979 Revolution.

provided evidence of the threat to Swiss investigators.[112]

The judge in charge of the case later stated "the investigations concluded that 13 people all holding diplomatic passports marked 'on mission' were closely involved in this matter,"[113] and that one or more official Iranian services were involved.[114] Police investigations found that two diplomats, introduced in the media as Samadi and Rezvani, were in Geneva during the crime, and left for Iran on a direct flight on the day of the assassination. The Swiss government issued international arrest warrants for them on June 15, 1990.[115]

The coordinator of this terrorist operation was Mohammad Mehdi Akhondzadeh Basti, who served as the general director for political and international relations in the

2 L'été

Tribune de Genève | Jeudi 9 juillet 2015

Espions à Genève (4/5)

L'assassinat de Kazem Radjavi

Les tueurs à la casquette bleue venaient d'Iran

Ahmad Moradi Talebi, un pilote déserteur, est abattu aux Pâquis en août 1987. En avril 1990, Kazem Radjavi est tombé dans un guet-apens à Tannay. Les deux meurtres sont signés. C'est une opération de la «Vavak», le service d'espionnage de la République islamique.

Olivier Bot

Quelques dates pour se repérer

Bullet riddled car of Professor Rajavi pictured in Tribune de Geneva, along with a story of his assassination in Switzerland.

Foreign Ministry. He had travelled to Switzerland several times in preparation for the attack.[116]

> The judge in charge of the case later stated "the investigations concluded that 13 people all holding diplomatic passports marked 'on mission' were closely involved in this matter.

On March 20, 2006, the examining magistrate in the Canton de Vaud district, Jacques Antenen, issued an international arrest warrant for Ali Fallahian, the Minister of Intelligence and Security in Rafsanjani's government, for his role in the assassination of Professor Rajavi.[117.] The thirteen Iranian diplomats are also wanted on charges of murdering Kazem Rajavi, to whom 162 members of Congress referred as "a great advocate of human rights, who had dedicated his life to the establishment of democracy in his homeland."[118]

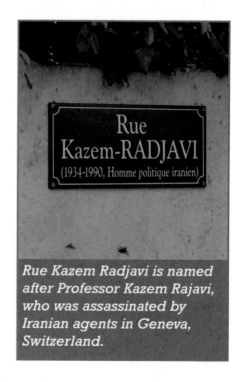

Rue Kazem Radjavi is named after Professor Kazem Rajavi, who was assassinated by Iranian agents in Geneva, Switzerland.

Turkey

Given its common border with Iran, the regime's embassy in Turkey has become one of Tehran's central diplomatic bases for dozens of terrorist operations in European countries. Those operations are in addition to other terrorist activities also taking place in Turkey. The *Washington Post* in November 1993 assessed that 50 Iranian dissidents had been assassinated in Turkey.[119] That number has increased dramatically over the past 15 years. In addition, the embassy provides support to the activities of the MOIS in the Balkans, particularly in Albania.

In 1988, ten MOIS agents, four of them carrying diplomatic passports, kidnapped Abolhassan Mojtahedzadeh, an MEK member, and took him to the consulate in Istanbul.[120]

Iran's embassy in Turkey.

Mojtahedzadeh was interrogated there for several days, and eventually placed in the trunk of the embassy car and driven towards the Iranian border. Only a few kilometers from the border, the car was stopped by Turkish police, who found Mojtahedzadeh in the trunk, foiling the plot.[121] The terrorists were arrested.

The regime's ambassador to Turkey, Manuchehr Mottaki, who later became foreign minister, was involved in the terrorist operation,[122] and was asked to leave Turkey by the Turkish government.[123] Mottaki, a veteran member of the IRGC's intelligence unit, had been involved in numerous assassinations on Turkish soil during his time as Ambassador.[124]

The regime's ambassador to Turkey, Manuchehr Mottaki, who later became foreign minister, was involved in the 1988 terrorist operation which targeted Abolhassan Mojtahedzadeh, an MEK member.

On March 14, 1990, Tehran unsuccessfully attempted to assassinate Mohammad Mohaddessin, chairman of the NCRI's Foreign Affairs Committee, in Istanbul. Hossein Mir Abedini, also of the NCRI's Foreign Affairs Committee, was badly injured by the terrorists during the attack.[125]

On June 4, 1992, Ali Akbar Ghorbani, a member of the MEK, was abducted in broad daylight in Istanbul.[126] His mutilated body was discovered on January 29, 1993 in a shallow grave in the suburbs of Istanbul. The Turkish Minister of the Interior declared that terrorists linked to Tehran were responsible for the killing.[127] On May

5, 1993, the People's Mojahedin released evidence that Ali Akbar Rafsanjani, the regime's president at the time, had personally ordered the victim's murder and that the terrorists had been trained in Sadiq Garrison in Qom.[128]

On June 5, the day after Ghorbani's kidnapping, a car belonging to another MEK member was rigged with explosives. Turkish police carried out a controlled detonation, and the bomb proved strong enough to shatter the glass of buildings in a radius of up to 200 meters.

On February 20, 1996, Zahra Rajabi, a member of the MEK's leadership council was assassinated in Istanbul. One of the assassins was Mohsen Karegar Azad, who worked as the Consular Secretary at the embassy in Turkey.

On February 20, 1996, Zahra Rajabi, a member of the MEK's leadership council, and Ali Moradi, an MEK supporter, were assassinated in Istanbul. Rajabi had gone to Turkey to help Iranian refugees.[129] She was shot five times at point blank range.[130] Moments later the terrorists killed Moradi and left the scene.[131] This terrorist operation was directed by the regime's embassy.[132] The NCRI identified one of the assassins as Mohsen Karegar Azad, who worked as the Consular Secretary at the embassy.[133]

On April 29, 2017, Said Karimian, director of GEM TV, was killed in Istanbul. Karimian was shot 27 times by a hit squad directed by the security services of the regime.[134]

Chapter Three

Iran's Terror Masterminds

Soon after the 1979 Revolution, the ruling regime began to enforce its grip on power by reining in, and then violently suppressing the secular opposition demanding democratic institutions. The domestic reign of terror was reflected outside Iran's borders by a foreign policy that used terror as a negotiating tool, and the extensive web of Iranian embassies, consulates and cultural/religious centers as its terrorist hubs. Opposition leaders and activists were kidnapped and/or killed by agents of the newly formed Quds Force, and Tehran's most effective intelligence agents, now veiled in diplomatic immunity, engineered and steered terror plots around the world.

Over the years, those terrorist-diplomats rose through the ranks and were rewarded for their assassinations and terror bombings with top government jobs and promotions to positions of influence and power within the regime's intelligence and security organs in both the so-called "moderate" and "hardline" administrations. As the following pages will reveal, the administration of Hassan Rouhani is no exception.

Reza Amiri Moqaddam

R eza Amiri Moqaddam, the head of the snake.

The key handler of terror ops abroad is the head of the MOIS Organization for Foreign Intelligence and Movements (OFIM), Reza Amiri Moqaddam (Moghadam). Intelligence stations abroad, and specifically those at the regime's embassies, are overseen by Amiri Moqaddam, considered one of the highest security officials of the regime. He reports directly to the Minister of Intelligence, currently Mahmoud Alavi.

Reza Amiri Moqaddam, a member of the IRGC, is the head of the MOIS Organization for Foreign Intelligence and Movements (OFIM) and the key handler of terror ops abroad. He was a central figure in the tripartite negotiations between Iraq, the U.S., and Iran in 2007-2008.

Amiri Moqaddam was a *pasdar*, a member of Iran's Islamic Revolutionary Guards Corps (IRGC), during the Iran-Iraq War in the 1980s. He was later transferred over to the Intelligence Ministry. He was the deputy for the Directorate of Foreign Intelligence and Movements prior to the re-organization of this entity, when it was elevated to the Organization for Foreign Intelligence and Movements.

During the years when American forces had an established presence in Iraq, Amiri Moqaddam was focused on operations against Coalition Forces there. During the tripartite negotiations between Iraq, the U.S., and Iran in 2007 and 2008, Amiri Moqaddam was a central figure in the regime's delegation. He negotiated with Ryan Crocker, then-U.S. ambassador to Iraq, as part of the regime's diplomatic delegation.[135]

Assadollah Assadi is the key MOIS agent in Europe. He has been responsible for coordinating Tehran's intelligence stations across Europe since his appointment in 2014.

Assadollah Assadi

Assadollah Assadi, station chief in Austria and coordinator of MOIS stations in Europe.

Assadollah Assadi is the key MOIS agent in Europe. As station chief in Vienna, the control center for MOIS stations in Europe for several years, he has been responsible for coordinating Tehran's intelligence stations across Europe since his appointment in 2014.

In view of the sensitive nature and significance of the attempted Paris bombing, its command was assigned to Assadi, a senior MOIS officer with special expertise in explosives and significant training in plotting terrorist operations, intelligence-gathering and surveillance.

Assadollah Assadi, arrested in Germany in July 2018 for his key role in a plot to bomb the Iranian Resistance's gathering in Paris was later extradited to Belgium. At the time of his arrest he was operating as a senior diplomat in Iran's Austrian embassy.

Assadi has been on assignment as the embassy's third secretary, working from the third floor of the Vienna embassy and reporting directly to Reza Amiri Moqaddam, the head of the Organization for Foreign Intelligence and Movements (OFIM).

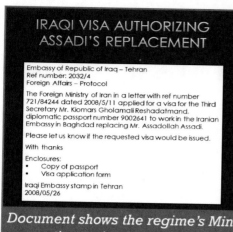

IRAQI VISA AUTHORIZING ASSADI'S REPLACEMENT

Embassy of Republic of Iraq – Tehran
Ref number: 2032/4
Foreign Affairs – Protocol

The Foreign Ministry of Iran in a letter with ref number 721/84244 dated 2008/5/11 applied for a visa for the Third Secretary Mr. Kiomars Gholamali Reshadatmand. diplomatic passport number 9002641 to work in the Iranian Embassy in Baghdad replacing Mr. Assadollah Assadi.

Please let us know if the requested visa would be issued.

With thanks

Enclosures:
• Copy of passport
• Visa application form

Iraqi Embassy stamp in Tehran
2008/05/26

Document shows the regime's Ministry of Foreign Affairs requesting a visa for the replacement for Assadi, confirming that Assadi was in Iraq until 2008 — the height of the bombings and killings in that country.

He was born in Khorramabad in the western province of Lorestan in 1971. He entered the MOIS following the Iran-Iraq War, starting in the provincial intelligence office in Khorramabad. One of his areas of focus at that time was the arrest and suppression of the MEK and other dissidents. He was later promoted and became involved in operations planning, specifically terrorist operations.

Assadi's resume is telling. Following the U.S. invasion of Iraq in 2003, he was appointed third consul in the Iranian embassy in Baghdad in early 2004. Assadi played a decisive role in terrorist plots, bombings and kidnappings in Iraq against Coalition Forces, the MEK, and Iraqi citizens from 2004 to 2008. He retained this position until mid-2008, after which he was replaced by an MOIS officer named Kiomars Reshadatmand (aka Haj Ali). A document in NCRI possession shows the regime's Ministry of Foreign Affairs requesting a visa for Reshadatmand as a replacement for Assadi, confirming that Assadi was in Iraq until 2008 — the height of the bombings and killings in that country.

Gholamhossein Mohammadnia

G holamhossein Mohammadnia, Tehran's Ambassador to Albania.

Although purportedly ambassador to Albania, Gholamhossein Mohammadnia's actual official post was deputy to the regime's intelligence minister for international

Ambassador to Albania until December 2018 when he was expelled for involvement in terrorist activities, Gholamhossein Mohammadnia's actual official post was deputy to the intelligence minister for international affairs. He was previously a permanent member of the regime's nuclear negotiations team.

affairs, when he was sent to Albania to design and oversee plots targeting the MEK in Albania. Mohammadnia was appointed at a meeting with the regime's president, Rouhani, on August 28, 2016.[136] The NCRI's Foreign Affairs Committee reported: "In 2016, Gholamhossein Mohammadnia, the MOIS deputy for international affairs and a member of the regime's delegation for nuclear negotiations with P5+1, was appointed as the regime's ambassador to Albania. As such, the embassy was placed under tighter control of the agents of the regime's intelligence service."[137]

On August 8, 2018, the NCRI revealed at a press conference in Brussels: "According to reports obtained from inside the regime, the Albanian affairs dossier has been handed over from the regime's Foreign Ministry to the Supreme National Security Council. Reza Amiri Moqaddam has been appointed to oversee the file. The regime's current ambassador in Albania, Gholamhossein Mohammadnia, has been the head of the international affairs office of the Ministry of Intelligence and Security (MOIS), an important section of the 'foreign office' or the Intelligence Organization for Foreign and Movements Affairs. Both he and Mostafa Roudaki, the head of the intelligence office of the regime's embassy in Albania, are veteran intelligence officers of the MOIS foreign intelligence department. Under the command of Reza Amiri Moqaddam, they are plotting and executing terrorist and intelligence operations against the MEK members residing in Albania."[138]

Some of the initiatives conducted by Mohammadnia in Albania include recruitment of MEK defectors in order to identify and gather intelligence about the MEK, as well as attempts to lure MEK members to defect. He has also hired local laborers for intelligence gathering. Mohammadnia additionally recruited people from Albania's neighboring countries, after which they were taken to Iran to receive training and prepare for terrorist operations and for their role in ongoing vilification campaigns against the MEK.

Mohammadnia was a permanent member of the regime's nuclear negotiations delegation and the talks that led to the signing of the Joint Comprehensive Plan of Action (JCPOA). He attended the negotiations using the name "Davoud Mohammadnia" and has been quoted in state-run media reports using Davoud as his first name. The MOIS typically would have issued him an alternate passport under that alias.

Mohammadnia conducted numerous interviews with the regime's media outlets regarding the nuclear negotiations. For example, he said during a December 7, 2014 interview: "From day one until two weeks ago, the talks that have taken place were all held in accordance with the views, awareness, guidance and red lines of the Leader [Khamenei], and revolved around the Islamic Republic's statehood tenets."[139]

Tehran's foreign ministry and embassies around the world play a key role in providing safe haven for its terrorists and their agenda.

Mohammadnia is a close friend of Foreign Minister Javad Zarif, with whom he attended several meetings with pro-Iran lobbies in the U.S. in 2006, when Zarif was Iranian ambassador to the UN.

Mohammadnia's presence in the nuclear negotiation across the table from P5+1 countries, added to Reza Amiri Moqaddam's presence in the negotiations with U.S. representatives pertaining to Iraqi affairs, clearly demonstrate that top-ranking intelligence operatives are fully collaborating with the regime's foreign ministry on common initiatives like the nuclear program and terrorism. Moreover, Tehran's foreign ministry and embassies around the world play a key role in providing safe haven for its terrorists and their agenda.

Mostafa Roudaki

Mostafa Roudaki, MOIS officer and first secretary of the regime's embassy in Albania.

In February 2018, the MOIS appointed a veteran officer, Mostafa Roudaki, as the first secretary of the Albanian embassy in line with its agenda to intensify the anti-MEK campaign by installing as many MOIS and Quds Force agents as possible. This plan went up a notch following complaints by the regime's Supreme Leader and other senior officials about the MEK's role in directing the nationwide uprisings. Roudaki was the second diplomat expelled on national security grounds by the Albanian government in December 2018.

An experienced officer of the Ministry of Intelligence and Security (MOIS), Roudaki entered Albania as first secretary, but in fact headed the regime's intelligence office in the embassy.

On February 5, 2018, the NCRI's Security and Counterterrorism Committee had revealed that "Mostafa Roudaki, who was in charge of the intelligence station at the regime's embassy in Austria in the early 2010's, returned to Iran in September 2014 and worked at the MOIS central headquarters. He had previously worked on the third floor in the regime's embassy in Austria, under the guise of a political advisor. At the conclusion of his mission in

Vienna, he was promoted to chief for intelligence stations in all European countries.

"Since the time he was in Austria, Mostafa Roudaki has been working on the MEK's case and has been in contact with a number of ex-MEK members (now working for the regime). In this regard, he made occasional trips to France. Roudaki pays ex-members to carry out the MOIS conspiracies against the MEK. Notorious MOIS agents such as Massoud Khodabandeh, Issa Azadeh and Ghorban Ali Hossein Nejad are in contact with him and support his activities."

Roudaki has also focused on recruiting local elements to gather information and intelligence against the MEK and to lay the groundwork for future acts of terrorism.

After Roudaki left his post as intelligence station chief in Vienna in September 2014, Assadollah Assadi became the head of the regime's intelligence outpost in Austria and the coordinator of the MOIS outposts in Europe. Assadi was also responsible for coordinating the network of the regime's intelligence operatives in Europe who were previously commanded by Roudaki.

Roudaki's close contacts with Assadi, arrested in 2018 by German police on charges of coordinating a terrorist bombing plot against a gathering in Villepinte near Paris, further demonstrates how the clerical regime uses its embassies, staffed with MOIS intelligence agents operating under the guise of diplomats, as a network to direct and coordinate terrorist operations all over the world.

Mohammad Ali Arzpeima Nemati

Mohammad Ali Arzpeima Nemati, Tehran's latest terrorist replacement.

Mohammad Ali Arzpeima Nemati was sent to Albania from Tehran around July 2018 to strengthen the regime's intelligence office. After the expulsion of his colleagues, Arzpeima Nemati spent about two weeks back in Tehran for briefing on ongoing operations, specifically those targeting the MEK, following which he returned to Tirana on December 30, 2018. (The expulsions were revealed on December 19. Mohammadnia and Roudaki landed at Tehran's Imam Airport on December 24.)

Arzpeima Nemati obscures his MOIS affiliations by describing himself to family and friends as an employee of the presidential office (a typical cover for MOIS agents), where he works under a pseudonym. His true identity papers identify him as the son of Hossein, residing in the Pirouzi district in eastern Tehran.

Chapter Four

Terrorists Promoted in Iran

Over the years, the regime in Tehran, righteously labeled as the world's leading state-sponsor of terrorism by the U.S. Government, has consistently commended and rewarded its terror agents, even those caught in the West, highlighting the extent to which terrorism has been institutionalized in the regime. A look at three examples is telling:

Mohammad Jafari Sahraroudi

After conducting terrorist operations in Austria, Brig. Gen. Mohammad Jafari Sahraroudi returned to Iran, where he rose rapidly within the ranks of the regime and has since occupied some of Tehran's most senior positions.

Sahraroudi commanded the hit squad dispatched to kill the Secretary General of the Democratic Party of Iranian Kurdistan (KDPI), Abdul Rahman Qassemlou, along with two of his colleagues, in Vienna on July 13, 1989. Sahraroudi was himself wounded during the assassination, which unfolded in the course of fabricated negotiations. He was unable to flee, and consequently arrested by Austrian police. A short time later, however, after enticements, threats, and intimidation tactics by the regime, Sahraroudi was freed due to "diplomatic immunity" and sent back to Iran.

IRGC Brig. Gen. Mohammad Jafari Sahraroudi, after conducting assassination of Abdul Rahman Qassemlou, in Austria in 1992, returned to Iran, where he has since occupied some of Tehran's most senior positions.

At the Austrian police's request, on December 22, 1989, an international arrest warrant was issued for Sahraroudi and two accomplices.

A commander during the regime's eight-year war with Iraq in the 1980s, Sahraroudi is instrumental in the regime's terrorism and export of fundamentalism. Following the U.S. invasion of Iraq in 2003, he played a significant role in organizing and overseeing terror cells and bombings in Iraq, as well as fueling the bloody sectarian conflict. During the presidency of Mahmoud Ahmadinejad, he was appointed deputy secretary for the domestic affairs office of the Supreme National Security Council (SNSC), where he specifically handled actions related to Iraq. During his tenure at the SNSC, he reported to Brig. Gen. Ali Larijani. After Larijani became the Speaker of Parliament, Sahraroudi became his aide and chief of staff. In these roles, he continued terrorist operations in Iraq.

During the presidency of Mahmoud Ahmadinejad, Mohammad Jafari Sahraroudi (1st, right) was appointed deputy secretary for the domestic affairs office of the Supreme National Security Council (SNSC), where he reported to Brig. Gen. Ali Larijani (2nd, right). After Larijani became the Speaker of Parliament, Sahraroudi became his aide and chief of staff.

For years, he has been using the name "Mohammad Jafari" to obscure his criminal terrorist background. For example, in a congratulatory message sent to several IRGC commanders in July 2016, he signed as "your brother, Brig. Gen. Mohammad Jafari, advisor and chief of staff for the office of the Speaker of Parliament."[140]

On August 13, 2017, Sahraroudi was put in charge of organizing Hassan Rouhani's presidential inauguration ceremony.

A recent report published by state-run media outlets said: "Dr. Mohammad Jafari, advisor and chief of staff for the Speaker of Parliament, who also sits on the board of directors of the Mellat House news agency [official parliament news outlet], met with Mellat House employees on the morning of Wednesday, September 12, 2018."[141]

Anis al-Naqqash

Anis al-Naqqash, born in Lebanon in 1951, is a terrorist well known for the hostage-taking of OPEC oil ministers in Vienna, Austria, in 1975. In 1980, the clerical regime dispatched Naqqash along with an Iranian, two other Lebanese nationals and two Palestinians to Paris to assassinate the Shah's last prime minister, Shapour Bakhtiar. The assassination failed, but there were two casualties, a female French neighbor and a police officer. Another police officer was permanently disabled.

(L-R) Mohsen Rafighdoust, Mohamed Salih al-Hosseini, Anis al-Naqqash, and Mohsen Rezaei – Beirut, 1980. Anis al-Naqqash, born in Lebanon in 1951, is a terrorist well known for the hostage-taking of OPEC oil ministers in Vienna, Austria, in 1975.

Six years later, Naqqash was freed in exchange for the freeing of 8 French hostages in Lebanon in a deal with the French government. Naqqash returned to reside in Iran. The clerical regime and the Islamic Revolutionary Guard Corps (IRGC) officially and openly conducted a public relations campaign to defend Naqqash and promote terrorism in official media outlets. Naqqash is now the head of the Amman Research Center and director of the Empowered Development of Middle East Communications Company.

On August 19, 2008, Naqqash said in an interview with the IRGC-affiliated Fars News Agency: "The decree to kill Bakhtiar was issued by the Revolutionary Court and the Imam [Khomeini] confirmed it. I told the IRGC friends that we have to act as soon as possible because [Bakhtiar] is a dangerous individual. But they had no intelligence or communication channels. I told them that I have operational experience and would accept the responsibility. I then went and conducted intelligence gathering. After two weeks, I returned to Iran and I told them that I had found Bakhtiar's residence and was even able to interview him. I crafted a comprehensive plan to execute Bakhtiar and began laying the groundwork for it. However, Mr. [Sadeq] Khalkhali [formerly the regime's Chief *Sharia* Justice] made a mistake and said in an interview that we had sent commandos to Paris to carry out the execution sentence of Shapour Bakhtiar. As a result, Bakhtiar refused to respond to my phone calls, refused to grant me an appointment to meet, and increased his security. That is how the meeting during which I was supposed to finish him got cancelled.

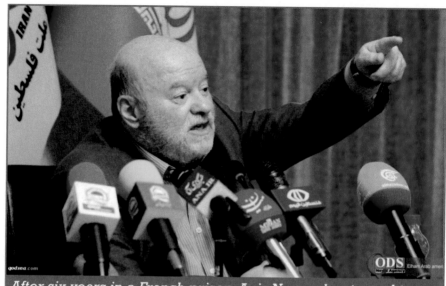

After six years in a French prison, Anis Naqqash returned to Iran where he is currently the head of the Amman Research Center and director of the Empowered Development of Middle East Communications Company.

"Meanwhile, they contacted me from Tehran and said that there were serious concerns there regarding a *coup d'état* and Bakhtiar must be killed as soon as possible. The decision was made for me; I believed it was necessary to do whatever it takes to finish the job. I procured a 7-mm gun with a silencer and went to see Bakhtiar. But they grew suspicious and did not open the building door for me. I immediately decided to fire at the lock and enter the building. But Bakhtiar's office door was bulletproof, so I could not do anything. One of the two bullets that struck me was fired from my own gun. I had fired at the door and the bullet ricocheted and hit me. Then I fought against the French police and was hit with another bullet before I was arrested."

In the same interview, Naqqash adds: "The terror plot basically was for me and two others to enter

Bakhtiar's office as reporters and kill him and the person accompanying him using a silencer without a sound. The plan was to prevent police officers patrolling in front of his house from noticing. However, unfortunately, as a result of Mr. Khalkhali's mistake and what he said, Bakhtiar was not granting interviews anymore and was not even answering our phone calls. Bakhtiar's security unit was increased. We then had to first kill the police officers at the front door and enter the residence by force. We were able to proceed until the door to Bakhtiar's office. But no matter how much we tried, we were unable to enter the room where Bakhtiar was."

In Iran, Naqqash attends various events organized by the clerical regime, including the eighth anniversary of the death of Emad Moqnieh, a former Hezbollah military commander, which took place in Tehran in February 2016. He attended along with Kazem Darabi, the terrorist involved in the Mykonos restaurant killings in Germany. Commanders of the IRGC were also seen among the crowd.

On October 28, 2018, Naqqash attended a press conference entitled "Bilateral Contributions of Iran and Palestine: Four Decades after the Islamic Revolution." He made pronouncements supportive of the meddling of the clerical regime in regional countries over the past 40 years.

Kazem Darabi

Kazem Darabi directed the hit squad which carried out the assassination on September 17, 1992, of four leaders of the Democratic Party of Iranian Kurdistan and other opponents of the regime at the Mykonos Restaurant in Berlin. Darabi was tried and sentenced to 15 years imprisonment in Berlin. He spent 10 years in prison, after which he was freed and returned to Iran on December 10, 2007. At the airport in Tehran on his return, he was warmly greeted by an official of the regime's Foreign Ministry.

Kazem Darabi directed the hit squad which carried out the assassination in 1992 of the Iranian dissidents in Berlin. Darabi was sentenced to 15 years imprisonment but he spent only 10 years in prison, after which he returned to Iran in 2007.

Darabi is but one example of the clerical regime's policy of rewarding terrorists who conduct terrorist acts outside Iran's borders, especially in western territories, with promotions and senior posts after they return to Iran.

In the 1980s, Darabi was an agent affiliated with

the regime's embassy in Germany, where he coordinated violent armed attacks on protests by Iranian opposition activists. In September 1992, he directed the terrorist operation at the Mykonos restaurant in Berlin involving several members of the Lebanese Hezbollah.

According to the Mykonos trial reports, Darabi was acting under the command of one of the regime's diplomats in the Iranian embassy in Germany, named Morteza Gholami. Gholami, an operative of the regime's Ministry of Intelligence and Security (MOIS), returned to Iran after the assassination. Darabi was also in contact with the regime's consul, Mohammad Amani Farani, in Berlin. Farani was also an intelligence operative.

After his return to Iran, Darabi was promoted to deputy head of the Lebanon Reconstruction Headquarters. This organization acts as a front for the IRGC Quds Force's

After his return to Iran, Darabi was promoted to deputy head of the Lebanon Reconstruction Headquarters. This organization acts as a front for the IRGC Quds Force's engineering unit.

engineering unit, which serves to rationalize the IRGC's extensive meddling in Lebanon.

The head of the Lebanon Reconstruction Headquarters is Brig. Gen. Hassan Shateri, aka Hessam Khoshnevis. Shateri was the Quds Force commander for engineering in Lebanon. He was killed by Syrian opposition forces on February 18, 2012, as he was returning to Beirut from Damascus.

In an interview with the IRGC-affiliated Fars News Agency on April 12, 2016, Darabi stated that he was a member of the Lebanon Reconstruction Headquarters. He was pictured with the flags of both the regime and the Lebanese Hezbollah, indicating his new role in the clerical regime.

Chapter Five

Terrorist Decision-Making in Tehran

According to the regime's mediaeval *sharia*, carrying out terrorist operations and spilling innocent blood require *fatwa* (religious decrees) issued by the *vali-e faqih* (Supreme Leader), currently Ali Khamenei. As such, acts of terror are facilitated, financed and directed at the highest levels, with the authorization of Supreme Leader Ali Khamenei himself.

Khamenei's more recent authorization for terrorist attacks on the MEK and Iranian Resistance came in the early days of 2018, when he stressed in a speech that the Iranian people's December-January uprising was organized by the MEK, vowing "this will not be without consequences."

Striking an ominous tone, the regime's top leader said, "We have to talk to the people who engaged in this saga based on emotions, whether they are students or non-students. But the case of the MEK is separate."

Prior to Khamenei's ultimatum on quashing the MEK's role in the uprisings, former IRGC Brig. Gen., Ali Shamkhani, currently the Secretary of the regime's Supreme National Security Council, threatened an "appropriate response" would be coming from an unexpected place.

Hence, the terrorist operations targeting the MEK on foreign soil were ordered by the highest authority in the religious dictatorship, Ali Khamenei, through his Special Affairs Office and the Supreme National Security Council, its highest decision-making body.

Role of Supreme Leader Ali Khamenei

All decisions on terrorist attacks abroad, particularly those targeting Iranian dissidents, require high levels of intelligence, coordination, logistics, and operational skills, as well as the political and diplomatic cover terrorist operatives need. But before all else, they need the approval of Supreme Leader Ali Khamenei. The Special Affairs Office of the Supreme Leader is the main body through which Khamenei provides such approvals and authorizations. This office is the apex of the pyramid of agencies which make up the terror apparatus.

Khamenei's role as the ultimate authority on terrorist operations outside Iran has been referenced in numerous international documents. Excerpts from Mykonos Trial Documents (translated from German) concerning the assassination of Dr. Sharafkandi in September 1992 in Berlin shed light on the role of Khamenei and his Special Affairs Office:

Execution operations are started in this Committee. When a decision is made to assassinate a person or a group, the Leader of the Revolution, as a political entity, endorses and approves the decision. As such, the Leader of the Revolution orders and assigns secret operations to kill people, without the creation of a court or a judgment. The targeted people that must be killed are either political opponents of the regime or

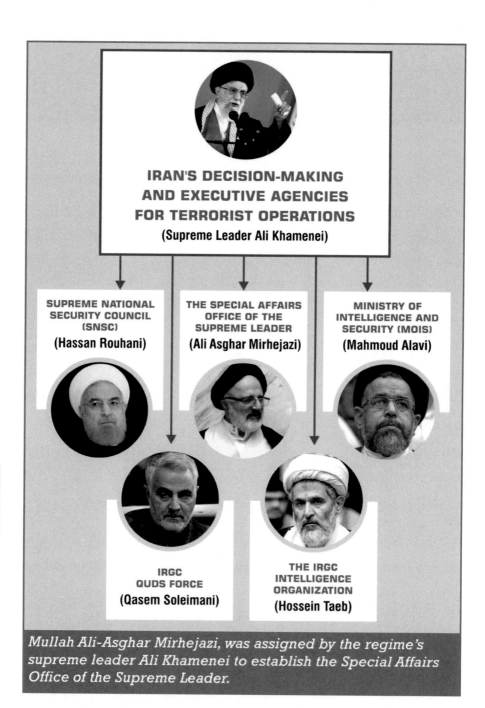

Mullah Ali-Asghar Mirhejazi, was assigned by the regime's supreme leader Ali Khamenei to establish the Special Affairs Office of the Supreme Leader.

are deemed as harmful by the regime. As a matter of principle, leaders of political parties and groups opposed to the regime are annihilated using this mechanism.

Excerpts from documents (translated from Italian) of the Criminal Court in Rome, Italy, regarding the assassination of Mohammad Hossein Naghdi, the NCRI's Representative in Italy, also emphasize Khamenei's role:

... The order to kill Mr. Naghdi was issued in a **fatwa** *by Khamenei, which must have been executed by the operations section of the Intelligence Ministry. On March 16, 1993, the operation against Naghdi was conducted and he was killed. ... The* **fatwa** *was handed down to the Special Affairs Committee. The Committee chose Mr. Fallahian to execute the order. He was a member of this Committee as well as the Minister of Intelligence and Security. ... Initially, there is a requirement for a series of intelligence. In this regard, Mr. Fallahian compiled his information through the Iranian embassy. The* **fatwa** *was issued from 1990 to 1991.*

In a 2001 investigative report entitled "Louis Freeh's Last Case" about the 1996 Khobar Tower bombing which killed 19 American servicemen, the *New Yorker* reveals that the bombing was authorized by Khamenei, writing: "...That same year, Saudi Crown Prince Abdullah met in Pakistan with the outgoing Iranian President, Hashemi Rafsanjani, and brought up the terrorist attack. 'We know you did it,' Abdullah told Rafsanjani, according to two people with knowledge of the conversation. Rafsanjani, in this account, insisted that he was not involved personally, but that if any Iranian had a role, 'it was he'—Ayatollah Khamenei, the country's supreme leader—and he pointed upward....

"The suspects confirmed their involvement in the bombing and described how the Iranians had ordered, supported, and financed the attack. Khassab, the cell member who had been turned over by the Syrians, claimed that he had met directly with Ahmad Sherifi [Sharifi], the Iranian Revolutionary Guard official who had selected the Khobar barracks as a target, and that Sherifi always announced that he was acting at the behest of Ayatollah Khamenei," added the *New Yorker*.

The Special Affairs Office of the Supreme Leader

Mullah Ali-Asghar Mirhejazi, was assigned by the regime's supreme leader Ali Khamenei to establish the Special Affairs Office of the Supreme Leader.

Following the death of the regime's founder, Ruhollah Khomeini, its newly appointed Supreme Leader Ali Khamenei appointed mullah Ali-Asghar Mirhejazi (also known as Mir-Hejazi and Mohammad Hejazi), then head of the Foreign Ministry's foreign office, to establish a special intelligence and security apparatus called the Special Affairs Office (aka Special Committee or Special Operations) to operate out of Khamenei's office. Mirhejazi was a core member of the Islamic Republic Party after Khomeini took power. When the Ministry of Intelligence was formed in 1984, he served as one of the deputies to Mohammad Reyshahri, the first Intelligence Minister.

> All terrorist operations are conducted under the supervision of the Special Affairs Office after Khamenei's personal approval.

The Special Affairs Office coordinates the regime's intelligence, security and terrorist organs. All terrorist operations are conducted under the supervision of the Special Affairs Office after Khamenei's personal approval. Considered as the highest intelligence and security authority, the Special Affairs Office is comprised of the Minister of Intelligence, Commander of the Quds Force, the head of the IRGC Intelligence Organization and the head of the IRGC Counter Intelligence Directorate. It has acted as the highest authority in intelligence, terrorist operations abroad and domestic oppression for the past three decades.

Khamenei heads the important decision-making sessions of this body; in his absence, Mirhejazi heads the sessions. All decisions by the Special Affairs Office are reported to Khamenei and implemented only after his approval. Intelligence ministers always work in coordination with this office, whose views bear weight on Khamenei's decision in appointing Intelligence ministers. (The president always appoints the Intelligence Minister with Khamenei's approval.)

Former Intelligence Minister Ali Fallahian always reported directly to Mirhejazi in addition to Ali Akbar Hashemi Rafsanjani, who was president at the time. Ghorbanali Dorri Najaf-Abadi and Ali Younesi (Intelligence ministers during Khatami's presidency) appointed their security directorates with the approval of Mirhejazi and his office. One notorious dispute between Khamenei and Ahmadinejad over the Intelligence minister came about because the minister took his orders from Mirhejazi rather than the president, Ahmadinejad. Khamenei rejected Ahmadinejad's objections.

Mirhejazi is also in direct contact with the IRGC commanders. Currently, Hossein Taeb, head of the IRGC Intelligence Organization (and a close associate of the Supreme Leader's son, Mojtaba Khamenei), takes his orders from Mirhejazi's office. IRGC Brigadier General Hossein Nejat, who heads the IRGC Counter Intelligence Directorate, operates under the supervision of the Special Affairs Office under Mirhejazi. His directorate is responsible for many politically-motivated arrests, particularly among high-ranking officials and military agencies.

Mullah Mirhejazi was added to the list of EU sanctions in March 2012 for his role in the widespread and severe violations of the Iranian people's civil rights. On May 30, 2013, his name was included in the list of U.S. sanctions as the Security Deputy to the Supreme Leader.[142]

Mykonos Trial Documents provide more details about the role of the Special Affairs Office:

The Special Affairs Committee makes the decisions.

[Former Intelligence Minister] Fallahian provides the findings of research and investigations to the Special Affairs Committee. This Committee was established to make decisions pertaining to important security affairs outside the jurisdiction of ministerial authorities and those which cannot be tabled at the

Supreme National Security Council due to their high sensitivity and urgency.

The establishment of this Committee is integral to the clerical system, or more aptly the vali-e faqih (Supreme Leader). This entity, which has not been referenced in the Constitution, has authorities beyond the government and the Majlis (parliament). Its membership includes: President, Minister of Intelligence and Security, Minister of Foreign Affairs, representatives of security, protection, military organizations and institutions, State Security Forces, among others.

The Leader of the Revolution in Iran is not an authority and leader for Muslims, but a new role created after the Islamic Revolution. Although this leader is a high-ranking cleric, he engages in political, not religious, affairs. The religious leadership still rests with religious leaders...

According to the prevalent mode of operation, the execution of decisions adopted at the Special Affairs Committee are assigned to an official present in decision-making sessions, who is deemed to be the most appropriate official in view of the target and the objectives and resources of the operation. This official then chooses a trusted individual that guides and executes the operation and is the so-called leader of the operations team. The team leader who meets all the requirements, i.e. is someone who has been involved in conflicts, is trained and has expertise, selects members of the operations team from among the best individuals according to his criteria. Field decisions at the time of executing the operation are within the purview of the team leader.

Other key decision-making and executive agencies for terrorism

Supreme National Security Council (SNSC)

The SNSC is the highest decision-maker in defense-security affairs. It is chaired by the president, currently Hassan Rouhani. Its standing members include the regime's Judiciary Chief, Speaker of Parliament, the Head of the Management and Planning Organization of Iran, the SNSC Secretary, the Representative of the Supreme Leader, the Second Representative of the Supreme Leader, the Chief of Staff for the Armed Forces, the IRGC Commander-in-Chief, the Commander-in-Chief of the Army, the Foreign Minister, the Intelligence Minister, and the Interior Minister. Decisions regarding the regime's

The regime's president, Hassan Rouhani, chairs the Supreme National Security Council, the highest decision-maker in defense-security affairs. Decisions regarding the regime's terrorist operations are adopted in the SNDC.

terrorist operations are adopted in the Supreme National Security Council.

Ministry of Intelligence and Security (MOIS)

The MOIS is the chief institution conducting the regime's terrorist operations abroad, especially in Western countries. The Foreign Affairs Committee of the National Council of Resistance of Iran (NCRI) published a comprehensive, detailed dossier in August 2018 regarding the role of MOIS stations in the regime's European embassies vis-à-vis terrorist operations, including the role of the MOIS itself in terrorism.

An entity within the Supreme National Security Council, the Intelligence Coordination Council, is supervised by the Intelligence Minister. It is composed of the Intelligence Minister, the Foreign Minister, the Interior Minister, the Head of the IRGC's Intelligence Organization, the Head of the IRGC's Intelligence Protection Organization, the Army's

> The MOIS is the chief institution conducting the regime's terrorist operations abroad, especially in Western countries.

Intelligence Deputy, the Head of the Army's Intelligence Protection Organization, the Commander of the State Security Forces (NAJA), the Head of NAJA's Intelligence Protection Organization, the Head of the Intelligence Protection Organization of the Defense Ministry, and the Head of the Intelligence Protection Organization of the Commander-in-Chief.

The Ministry of Intelligence and Security (MOIS) office responsible for conducting extraterritorial terrorist operations, particularly on European and American soil, is called the Organization for Foreign Intelligence and Movements (OFIM). The status of OFIM was upgraded in the beginning of 2017 from a directorate to an organization. Based on the regime's usual procedures, when such an upgrade takes place, new sectors are created, personnel and budgets are increased, and decisions are taken and implemented more fluidly. MOIS stations abroad, and specifically those at the regime's embassies, are tied to OFIM. One of the tasks assigned to OFIM was the expansion of intelligence stations in different countries.

> The Quds Force uses foreign agents in countries in which it has influence, such as members of the Lebanese Hezbollah, to conduct its terrorist operations.

The head of OFIM, Reza Amiri Moqaddam, reports directly to the Minister of Intelligence, currently Mahmoud Alavi.

IRGC Quds Force

The extraterritorial Quds Force was created by the IRGC to meddle in the affairs of regional neighbors; it serves as the IRGC's arm for terrorist operations and warmongering. The Quds Force has conducted many terrorist operations, particularly after 2009, in various countries in the Western Hemisphere, Europe, Asia and Africa.

The Quds Force in turn created a separate unit for terrorist operations called Unit 400, which is responsible for the provision of military support, training and guidance to terrorist agents and guerilla organizations in various parts of the world. The Quds Force uses foreign agents in countries in which it has influence, such as members of the Lebanese Hezbollah, to conduct its terrorist operations.

Quds Force commander Qassem Soleimani was a commander of the Islamic Revolutionary Guard Corps (IRGC) during the Iran-Iraq War in the 1980s. He was appointed as the Quds Force commander in 1997. Less than a year later, major bombings occurred in Kenya and Tanzania, resulting in hundreds of casualties. In 2010, he was promoted to the rank of major general by the regime's Supreme Leader, Ali Khamenei, for his activities in Iraq and Afghanistan.

Soleimani oversees all Quds Force operations in neighboring and other Middle East countries, the Far East

Quds Force commander Qassem Soleimani (the person in the middle) was a commander of the IRGC during the Iran-Iraq War in the 1980s.

and other Asian and African countries. He also oversees export of fundamentalism and terrorism to Europe and the Americas. During his tenure as Quds Force commander, the Quds terrorist network has experienced a secret expansion in Latin America, the Gulf states, Palestine, Afghanistan, Turkey, Iraq, Turkmenistan, Kazakhstan, Tajikistan and other Muslim former-Soviet republics.

Soleimani is regarded as a close confidant to Khamenei and is trusted by him. He is also Khamenei's special advisor for regional affairs, including Iraq, Syria, Yemen, Afghanistan, Lebanon and Palestine.

Operations conducted by the Quds Force over the past decade include:

A Saudi diplomat, Hassan al-Qahtani, was gunned down while driving in the Pakistani city of Karachi on May 16, 2011. The attack was conducted by the Quds Force in reaction to, and two months after, the involvement of Saudi military forces in Bahrain. The terror squad was comprised of two assassins riding a bike. Four days prior to the assassination, two grenades were thrown at the Saudi consulate gate in Karachi.

In 2011, the Quds Force planned a bombing at a restaurant in Washington D.C., which regularly hosted the former Saudi ambassador to the U.S., Adel al-Jubeir. The operation was organized by an Iranian-American, Mansour Arbabsiar, who had been recruited by the Quds Force, and involved local criminals of Mexican origin. The operation was neutralized after Arbabsiar's arrest on September 29, 2011. During investigations, Arbabsiar revealed that the Quds Force was also planning to assassinate the Saudi and Israeli ambassadors to Argentina as well as the Israeli ambassador to the U.S.

In 2012, the Quds Force's Unit 400 orchestrated an operation against a foreign embassy in the Thai capital Bangkok. In accordance with the plan, the Quds Force sent its agents to Thailand to obtain explosives and gather intelligence regarding the targets. The plot was foiled as a result of an accidental explosion during the making of the bomb at a residential unit rented by Quds Force agents. After the accidental explosion, three Iranians were arrested in Thailand: Mohammad Khazai, Saeed Moradi, and Ali Akbar Norouzi. Another Iranian national involved in the plot, Massoud Sedaqatzadeh, escaped to Malaysia, but was arrested at the Kuala Lumpur airport upon arrival.

In June 2012, Kenyan police announced the arrests of two Quds Force operatives: Ahmad Abolfathi and Seyyed Mansour Moussavi. The two belonged to Unit 400. The suspects turned over 15 kg of explosives to authorities, which they had hidden in Mombasa to carry out terrorist attacks against western interests in Kenya. During their interrogations, they confessed that they had received orders from their commanders to target representative offices of the U.S., Britain, Israel and Saudi Arabia. They were sentenced to life in prison in Kenya.

In June 2016, German authorities revealed the arrest of a Pakistani national on charges of spying for the Iranian regime. The Associated Press identified him as Haidar Syed Mustafa and reported he had been detained in the northern German city of Bremen. On March 17, 2017, German prosecutors sentenced him to four years and three months in prison on charges of spying for the IRGC's Quds Force. He was receiving 2,052 Euros per month from his superiors.

On January 16, 2018, on the orders of the German federal prosecutor's office, German special forces conducted a series of raids in connection with 10 spies tied to the IRGC's Quds Force in various German provinces. The raids led to arrests. Investigations were carried out in the states of Berlin, Baden-Wuerttemberg, North Rhine-Westphalia, and Bavaria.

IRGC Intelligence Organization (IIO)

The IRGC's Intelligence Organization (IIO) was created in June 2009, four months after the start of the 2009 uprisings, as a result of the amalgamation of IRGC intelligence and a number of other intelligence-related bodies within the IRGC. The head of the Organization is Hossein Taeb, previously commander of the *Bassij* Resistance force. The Organization functions in coordination with the office of Khamenei, who has direct supervision of it, and plays a role both in domestic suppression and terrorist activities abroad. In Iran, the Organization uses the *Bassij* Organization to gather intelligence and conduct surveillance against all sectors of Iranian society.

Mullah Hossein Taeb, is the head of the IRGC Intelligence Organization (IIO), previously commander of the Bassij Resistance force.

There are three different intelligence organizations within the Islamic Revolutionary Guard Corps (IRGC): the IRGC Intelligence Organization (IIO), the IRGC Counter Intelligence Organization, and the IRGC Protection Organization. All three have their own particular responsibilities and modus operandi, and operate directly or indirectly under the supervision of Supreme Leader Ali Khamenei and the IRGC's Commander-in-Chief, Mohammad-Ali Jafari.

The IRGC Intelligence Organization has evolved into the pillar of the IRGC in all 31 provinces. Other directorates and units of the IRGC have been ordered to coordinate their activities with the IIO, and to provide reports about their activities and intelligence collected to it.

The heads of IIO in each province are approved and appointed by Khamenei. Ta'eb is in close coordination with the IRGC Commander in Chief and the chief of staff of Khamenei's representatives in the IRGC. The IRGC

Intelligence Organization does not answer to the President. The *Majlis* has no authority to summon its head for questioning.

In December 2016, Brig. Gen. Mohammad Hossein Zibaee-nejad, aka Hossein Nejat, was appointed as the deputy head of the IRGC Intelligence Organization. Nejat was an IRGC commander during the Iran-Iraq war and one of the founders of the IIO. During Mahmoud Ahmadinejad's first term as president, Nejat was deputy for internal security to the Supreme National Security Council and was, for a time, commander of Khamenei's security detail.

The IIO is a crack unit, with 2,000 agents in the IIO headquarters in Tehran and 2,000 agents in the provinces.

All intelligence agencies, including those in the Quds Force, the Ground Forces, the *Bassij*, the Air Force and the Navy, have come under the supervision of the IIO, and Hossein Ta'eb has assumed unrivalled authority. To undermine the power of the IIO, IRGC Commander in Chief Jafari created a Strategic Directorate within the IRGC. Presently, all planning by the Quds Force, Ground Forces, the Air Force

> The IRGC's Intelligence Organization (IIO) functions in coordination with the office of Khamenei, who has direct supervision of it.

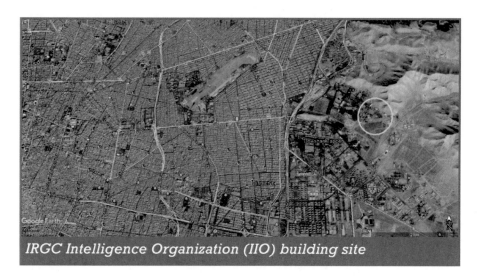

IRGC Intelligence Organization (IIO) building site

and the Navy is under the supervision of the Strategic Directorate, which also directs the IRGC's intelligence directorates in all its branches. Jafari is the head of this

IRGC Intelligence Organization (IIO): 1-Command, 2- Mess Hall, Diner, 3- Prayer Hall, 4- Foreign Intelligence, code number 800, 5- Building 800, 6- Building 500 (Counter-espionage), 7- Planning 400, 8- Internal Directorate 1300, 9-Internal Directorate 1300, 10- Documentation Center, 11- Security Directorate, 12- Logistics, 13- Defense Directorate, 14- Kolbeh or Cottage, (Intelligence-gathering), 15- Psychological Directorate 600, 16- Surplus for other directorates

directorate, which does macro planning on an annual basis.

The Central Headquarters of the IIO in Tehran was initially located in the Iranian Army's equestrian buildings, constructed during the time of the Shah (Do-Kouhe HQ located between the IRGC HQ and the Mohammad Rassoulallah Division). With the transfer of Navy HQ to Bandar Abbas, the IIO added the buildings of the Navy HQ in Do-Kouhe and the IRGC's Protocol Center (adjacent to the office of the Supreme Leader's Representative in the IRGC). The following aerial photo shows the exact locations.

Chapter Six

IRGC and MOIS, Terror Partners

The Iranian regime can be described as a military-police dictatorship. The IRGC is the main instrument of armed suppression, and the Ministry of Intelligence and Security (MOIS) is the primary security apparatus. The MOIS was born out of the IRGC, and its role in suppressing the Iranian people domestically and exporting terrorism abroad complements that of the IRGC. The two entities, despite differences that they have on many occasions, are interlinked and jointly conduct domestic repression and terrorist operations outside Iran.

The IRGC as the MOIS' Godfather

The Ministry of Intelligence and Security (MOIS) was founded in 1984 as the result of the amalgamation of several intelligence institutions established after the Shah's overthrow in 1979. The IRGC was founded at the time of the regime's establishment, as was the IRGC's internal intelligence unit, known as the IRGC Intelligence Organization. When the Iranian regime sought to centralize intelligence services into a single entity, the Ministry of Intelligence took shape from within the IRGC's intelligence unit, which acted as its foundation and skeleton.

Former IRGC Commander Mohsen Rezai (second from left) who was the original founder of the IRGC intelligence unit in 1979, explained how the MOIS had been founded thanks to the IRGC's intelligence service.

Mohsen Rezaei, IRGC Commander during the Iran-Iraq War period and a founder of the IRGC intelligence unit in 1979, explained how the MOIS had been founded thanks to the IRGC's intelligence service at a meeting on July 14, 2010 at his residence in Tehran. Officials of the IRGC's intelligence unit from 1981 to 1983 present at the meeting included Majid Alavi, Reza Javadi, Hossein Khorasani, Houshang Taheri, and Mohammad-Hossein Assadi.

Rezai stated: "In early 1984, there was murmuring that intelligence should be separated from operations. Discussions began and meetings were held. ... In the end, on September 23, 1984, on the orders of the *Imam* (Ruhollah Khomeini), we separated the intelligence unit from the IRGC and gave it to our new friends. The only thing that they did was to change the name on the sign from IRGC to 'Ministry of Intelligence and Security.' We transferred 95 percent of the organizational capacity, human resources, entities and even locations. ... I gave all the (IRGC) intelligence facilities, in which we had made a ton of investments, along with all the good intelligence agents who were some of my best and closest friends in the IRGC, to Mr. Reyshahri (Mohammad Reyshahri was the first Minister of Intelligence)."

Majid Alavi added: "You handed over the entire IRGC intelligence unit, one hundreds percent of it. You indicated 95 percent, but I believe 100 percent, because in all honesty, the people that remained in the IRGC intelligence unit were not the original members."

Thus, the core apparatus and fundamental components of the MOIS were formed out of the IRGC's intelligence unit, including its former agents, torturers and criminals.

Ministry of Intelligence in the cabinet

The IRGC is directly under the control of the Supreme Leader, Ali Khamenei. The Ministry of Intelligence is part of the cabinet and is supposed to be under the control of the regime's president. However, at the top, the Ministry of Intelligence as well as the Ministry of Foreign Affairs are in close contact with the Supreme Leader. In other words, these two agencies are subject to the Supreme Leader approval when it comes to pursuing their policies. On the other hand, key MOIS officials were brought in from the IRGC.

Majid Alavi: Swinging between MOIS and IRGC

One example of an IRGC official who rose to the top of the MOIS hierarchy is IRGC Brig. Gen. Majid Alavi. In recent years, he has been transferred back from the MOIS and re-appointed to the IRGC's Quds Force. He has commanded numerous terrorist operations on foreign soil.

As an official of the IRGC's intelligence unit, Alavi was involved in the torture and interrogation of political prisoners in 1981. He later became an MOIS agent for foreign operations and operated for eight years in Sudan and Saudi Arabia as a secret agent. His identity was revealed in Sudan and he returned to Tehran.

When Ali Akbar Hashemi Rafsanjani was president and Ali Fallahian was the regime's Intelligence Minister, Majid Alavi was head of the Arab section of MOIS's foreign affairs division. Mostafa Pourmohammadi was chief of the foreign affairs division at the time. One of the mandates of this office related to the Palestinian Islamic Jihad and the Lebanese Hezbollah.

After the "chain killings" of intellectuals in Iran were exposed in 1999, Pourmohammadi, who had direct involvement in the killings, along with other individuals, including Alavi, left the MOIS and created a parallel special intelligence organization in the Supreme Leader's office under the guidance of Ali Asqar Mirhejazi. During this period, Alavi became a close business partner of Mirhejazi.

After Mahmoud Ahmadinejad became president in 2005, and Mohseni Ejei became his Intelligence Minister, Alavi was appointed MOIS foreign operations chief on the recommendation of Mirhejazi.

In July 2009, Ahmadinejad removed Ejei and replaced him with Alavi as Acting Intelligence Minister. The translation of the text of Ahmadinejad's decree follows:

> *In the Name of God,*
>
> *Mr. Majid Alavi,*
>
> *Greetings,*
>
> *In view of your commitment, competency, and valuable experience, on the basis of this decree, you are appointed as Acting Minister of Intelligence.*
>
> *You are hereby obliged to oversee the work of the ministry's deputies and managers, and to organize the affairs of the ministry and provide reports to me until the Islamic Consultative Assembly (parliament) approves a vote of confidence and the new minister is appointed.*
>
> *It is my hope that along with coordinating and cooperating with members of the cabinet and executing the assigned legal authorities, you will be successful in carrying out the Islamic system's goals.*
>
> *Mahmoud Ahmadinejad."*

In March 2011, Khamenei's Special Intelligence Office decided to operationalize terrorist strategies outside of Iran. Majid Alavi was reassigned from the MOIS to Unit 400 of the Quds Force. On the basis of his familiarity with foreign affairs and especially with the affairs of Arab countries, he became responsible for coordinating with Hezbollah, Hamas, and the Islamic Jihad. He was also responsible for operations in Southeast Asia and Oceania.

Thai police escort Iranian bomb suspect Mohammad Kharzei during an investigation at his rented house in Bangkok, Feb. 20, 2012.

On February 14, 2012, several bombs exploded in the Thai capital Bangkok. One of the bombers, an Iranian national named Saeed Moradi, lost both his legs when the bomb accidentally exploded, and several others were injured. Mohammad Khazai, 42, was arrested at an airport after fleeing Thailand. Another suspect, Massoud Sedaqatzadeh, 31, escaped to Malaysia on the day of the incident, but was arrested as he was boarding a plane destined for Tehran.

A fourth operative, Mehrdad Madani, was arrested by the police on the evening of February 26, 2012, when his residence was raided. The police had identified the suspects after investigating the SIM cards of their mobile devices. Subsequent investigations by Thai security officials revealed that seven Iranian operatives were involved in the Bangkok bombing plot. They also showed that on January 19, another Iranian national had entered Bangkok

Saeid Moradi had his legs blown off after a grenade he hurled bounced back onto him, as police closed in on him outside a Bangkok school on February 14, 2012. He is currently in prison for life in Thiland.

under the pseudonym Hosssein Tehrani. Security officials believed that this was none other than Majid Alavi. Alavi left Bangkok several days later. However, his short visit was enough to raise suspicions among security officials that a terrorist plot might be in the making.

According to reports obtained in recent years, Brig. Gen. Majid Alavi has been transferred to Syria and is acting as one of the deputies of Brig. Gen. Seyyed Javad Ghaffari, the IRGC's commander in Syria.

Mullah Hossein Taeb: Former MOIS Deputy and Current IRGC Intelligence Chief

Mullah Hossein Taeb is the current head of the IRGC Intelligence Organization. He was born in 1963, became a member of the IRGC in 1982, operating in Tehran's tenth district. He was intimately involved in suppressing and interrogating members and supporters of the main opposition Mujahedin-e Khalq (MEK) and other political opponents.

Taeb was for some time the head of the intelligence and operations unit of the First Corps of the so-called Sarollah Base. He was later transferred from IRGC to MOIS following the latter's formation.

Taeb was a contemporary of Khamenei's son, Mojtaba, studying at the same time as a cleric, which is how he came to know Khamenei. He climbed the ranks during the tenure of Intelligence Minister Ali Fallahian and was appointed as deputy for counter-intelligence. His pseudonym in the MOIS is Meysam.

The 1994 bombings at the Imam Reza Shrine in Mashhad, designed and conducted by the MOIS when Taeb was

From left to right: Mohammad Reza Naghdi, Commander of IRGC's Bassij paramilitary force; Hossein Taeb, Head of the IRGC's Intelligence Organization; and IRGC Commander Major General Mohammad Ali Jafari

a deputy minister, are one of the most infamous plots orchestrated by Taeb during his tenure in MOIS. Resulting in 26 deaths and over 370 injuries, the bombings were intended to cause widespread hatred of the MEK, whom regime officials falsely blamed for the bloodbath, with the goal of putting pressure on western countries to cut contacts with the MEK and expel them from their territories.

The 1994 killings of three Christian pastors (Bishop Haik Hovsepian Mehr, Bishop Mehdi Dibaj, and Reverend Tateos Michaelian) occurred according to plans personally drawn up by Taeb. Once again, a prepared and phony televised scenario was broadcast by state-run media blaming the MEK for the plot.

Taeb was also a chief executor of the chain killings of 1998. He was removed from office as a result of factional feuding, but later promoted to Khamenei's office. He played an active role along with Khamenei's son, Mojtaba, in setting up a parallel intelligence service operating out of Khamenei's office.

Taeb was also responsible for suppressing the student uprising of July 9, 1999, when he was acting as the intelligence chief of the IRGC. He ordered the arrest of students identified by the IRGC's intelligence unit.

In 2000, Taeb carried out Khamenei's orders to create a fascist entity called Bonyad Isargaran in order to organize and rally some of the regime's torturers, criminals and suppressive forces.

In 2005, Taeb was appointed as the head of the IRGC's paramilitary Bassij Force on the recommendation of Mojtaba Khamenei. He sought to organize the Bassij to stuff ballot boxes with Ahmadinejad's name in order to meet the demands of Khamenei.

In October 2009, after the IRGC's intelligence directorate became the IRGC Intelligence Organization, Taeb was appointed as its head, a post he continues to hold.

Policy Recommendations

T he surge in Tehran's terror and espionage on Western soil has set off alarm bells in European capitals and the U.S. Nonetheless, to date the diplomatic and law enforcement responses have been tepid. Although several agents were arrested on terrorism and espionage-related charges in the U.S. and Europe in 2018, one top terrorist-diplomat is in prison, and five others, including an ambassador, were expelled, a multilateral Western approach to Tehran's rogue behavior remains elusive.

Western capitals have reached a consensus on the need for pragmatic, effective and pro-active measures and policy to counter the Iranian regime's terrorism around the world. There is also a global consensus that Tehran's unbridled terrorism and other malevolent actions are by-products of its extremist, suppressive, and expansionist nature. Unfortunately, there is less evidence of agreement on a robust policy to counter the regime.

Even the most punishing and best-implemented counter-terrorism measures, while effective in diminishing Tehran's capacity for terror and mayhem, will not change the nature of the regime. The theocratic dictatorship is intrinsically incapable of reform and lacks both the will and the intent to do so. For these very reasons, the imperative of a change of regime in Tehran is not an ideological or political preference, but an indispensable prerequisite to liberate Iran, its people, and the region from the decades-long cycle of death, destruction, and instability. Any effective, meaningful policy must start by recognizing the inalienable and legitimate right of the Iranian people to overthrow the theocratic regime.

As discussed extensively in this report, the Islamic Revolutionary Guard Corps (IRGC), along with the Ministry of Intelligence and Security (MOIS) and their affiliate organizations, are two key components of Iran's violent suppression of Iranians inside Iran, international terrorism and regional destabilization, as well as assassination of dissidents abroad. The following steps are, therefore, essential to compelling Iran's ruling regime to curb its domestic and foreign terrorism:

> The U.S. State Department designated the IRGC as a Foreign Terrorist Organization in April 2019. The IRGC's subordinate branches and affiliate entities also meet the criteria for the FTO designation as set forth in section 219 of the Immigration and Nationality Act (8 U.S.C. 1189) . The United States should fully implement the FTO designation to ban members, affiliates, and agents of the IRGC from entering the United States. Full implementation should also lead to the prohibition of individuals or organizations providing material support or resources to the IRGC and all its subordinate branches and affiliated organizations.

> The U.S. State Department should also designate the Ministry of Intelligence and Security (MOIS) as a Foreign Terrorist Organization. The MOIS and all

> Any effective, meaningful policy must start by recognizing the inalienable and legitimate right of the Iranian people to overthrow the theocratic regime.

its subordinate branches meet the criteria for the FTO designation as set forth in section 219 of the Immigration and Nationality Act (8 U.S.C. 1189): The MOIS is a foreign organization that engages in terrorism or terrorist activities or has the capability and intent to engage in terrorism or terrorist activity by means of its global network and by providing support for FTO designated entities; further, its terrorism or terrorist activities threaten the national security of the United States or the security of American nationals.

The MOIS "provides financial, material, or technological support for, or financial or other services to Hizballah and Hamas," both FTO designated. The MOIS "has facilitated the movement of al Qa'ida operatives in Iran and provided them with documents, identification cards, and passports."[143] In 2018 alone, several MOIS senior officials and agents were arrested in Albania, Germany, France, Belgium, the Netherlands, Denmark, and the United States for terrorism and espionage related charges. Previously, the MOIS was implicated in terror operations in Germany and Argentina by the judicial systems of the two countries. The MOIS in 2018 clearly threatened the United States and its nationals by targeting U.S. nationals in Albania, France, and the United States, among them many former and current American officials. Although the United States has already designated the MOIS as Specially Designated Global Terrorists (SDGT), the FTO designation would ban members, affiliates, and agents of the MOIS from entering the United States. FTO designation also triggers a prohibition on individuals or organizations providing material support or resources to these organizations. The significant surge in terrorist and espionage operations by the MOIS across Europe and the United States in 2018 warrants its designation as an FTO without further delay.

➤ Europe should also blacklist the IRGC and the MOIS and all their subordinate branches. Anything short of that will only embolden the regime to double down on its espionage and terrorist activities in Europe and elsewhere. A comprehensive, multilateral effort including European allies and other key nations in line with multinational efforts on sanctions against the Iranian regime, are key to checking that regime's terrorism. Building international partnerships toward this goal should remain a priority.

➤ Tehran's terrorist diplomats should be brought to justice or expelled, and its embassies shut down. They have been and remain the nerve centers of espionage and terrorism and critical to Tehran's terrorist operations abroad. Albania has been the first European nation to expel Tehran's ambassador on terrorism charges and should now lead the way by closing the Iranian regime embassy in Tirana.

> The agents and operatives of the regime's intelligence services and the IRGC should be legally prosecuted and/or expelled from the U.S. and Europe.

> The United States and Europe must make clear to Tehran that they will not tolerate continued violent suppression of rightful demonstrations in the streets of Iran and will hold members of the IRGC, MOIS, and the Judiciary responsible for crimes against participants in such demonstrations.

> The United States, European nations and their allies must ensure the safety of Iranians abroad, and particularly Iranian dissidents, from harm and violence by the IRGC, MOIS and their affiliates.

> The above recommendations should be decisively implemented to pressure Tehran to stop its export of terrorism and its use of diplomatic facilities around the world as terror hubs. Most importantly, doing so would send a positive message to the Iranian people, as they seek fundamental change for a free, democratic, and non-nuclear republic in Iran.

THE WALL STREET JOURNAL

October 31, 2018

Bags of Cash and a Bomb Plot: Inside a Covert Iranian Operation in Europe

Europeans have tried to salvage the Iran nuclear deal, but an alleged plan to launch an attack near Paris is jeopardizing their support

Belgian authorities said they stopped an Iranian émigré and his wife on their way to a June 30 conference in Villepinte, France, and found a device that contained a powerful explosive. PHOTO: REGIS DUVIGNAU/REUTERS

By Matthew Dalton

On a sunny day in late June, an Iranian émigré named Amir Saadouni met on the terrace of a Luxembourg cafe with an Iranian intelligence agent known to him only as Daniel, who for years had paid him to spy on a France-based group that opposes the regime in Tehran.

Gathering information "isn't enough for us," Daniel said, according to people familiar with the matter. They said the agent gave Mr. Saadouni and his wife an explosive device to set off at an annual conference organized by the group, where Rudy Giuliani, President Trump's lawyer, was due to speak on June 30.

European security services, acting in part on a tip provided by Israeli intelligence, were watching, officials said. Belgian authorities said they stopped Mr. Saadouni and his wife on their way to the conference outside Paris, and found a device that contained half a kilogram of TATP, a powerful explosive. German police arrested the intelligence agent a few miles from the border with Austria, where he was stationed as a diplomat at the Iranian embassy and would have enjoyed immunity from prosecution, officials said.

The alleged plot was thwarted at a crucial diplomatic moment, a month after Washington withdrew from the Iran nuclear accord. French President Emmanuel Macron and other European leaders are trying to salvage the deal. On Nov. 5, the Trump administration is set to impose a new round of sanctions—its toughest yet targeting Iran's oil sector.

The allegation that an Iranian operative plotted an attack on French soil is jeopardizing Europe's support for the accord. As U.S. and Israeli officials ramp up pressure on Europe to sever ties with Tehran, they have cited it as a reason why Mr. Macron and other leaders should end their support for the deal.

On Tuesday, Denmark announced it had foiled an Iranian operation to kill a dissident, turning up the pressure on Europe to harden its posture toward Tehran. A spokesman for Iran's foreign ministry said Iran had no involvement in the case.

This account of the alleged June plot is based on interviews with European officials as well as people close to Mr. Saadouni and his wife, Nasimeh Naami. An attorney for the agent, identified as Assadollah Assadi, declined to comment. The Iranian government didn't respond to a request for comment. Iranian Foreign Minister Javad Zarif has claimed the plot was mounted by Iran's international opponents to drive a wedge between Tehran and the West.

Given France's role in trying to salvage the deal, some European authorities thought the alleged plot might be a rogue operation. But French authorities said they traced responsibility for it to a senior official in the Iranian

intelligence ministry, Saeid Hashemi Moghadam.

Now, officials and analysts express concern the incident marks an escalation in Iran's willingness to undertake violent covert operations in the West—after years of relative restraint—as diplomacy with the U.S. falters.

"They feel the constraints on them have been removed," said Bruce Riedel, a senior fellow at the Brookings Institution, a Washington-based think tank, and former official at the Central Intelligence Agency, the White House and the Pentagon.

The Iranian government and the group targeted in the alleged plot, known as Mujahedin-e Khalq, or MEK,

Rudy Giuliani, President Trump's lawyer, addressed the June 30 conference near Paris.
PHOTO: REGIS DUVIGNAU/REUTERS

have been foes since the country's Islamic revolution in 1979. MEK was one of several factions vying for power and, after losing a bloody struggle with forces loyal to Ayatollah Ruhollah Khomeini, it was largely forced into exile, though it maintained a clandestine membership inside Iran. The U.S. government considered MEK a terrorist organization from 1997 to 2012, when the

Obama administration lifted that designation.

Mr. Saadouni, who is 38 years old, was granted political asylum in Belgium as a member of MEK after leaving Iran roughly a decade ago. He quickly settled into life in the West, cultivating an interest in rock music and dressing in black, people who know him say. His favorite bands included Rammstein and Pink Floyd.

He also struck up an online relationship with Ms. Naami, who worked at a swimming pool in Iran. Ms. Naami came to Belgium and married Mr. Saadouni.

Several years ago, Mr. Assadi, under the alias Daniel, approached Mr. Saadouni saying he was an Iranian intelligence agent seeking information about MEK, according to people close to the couple.

Though he bore the nondescript title of "Third Counselor at the Iranian embassy in Vienna," French officials say Mr. Assadi was working for Iran's intelligence ministry, which is controlled by hard-liners and often takes orders directly from Iran's Supreme Leader Ayatollah Ali

Khamenei. Mr. Assadi was prepared to pay thousands of euros for the intelligence, a person close to Mr. Saadouni said, and threatened to make life difficult for Mr. Saadouni's family in Iran if he refused.

Starting around 2014, Mr. Saadouni and Ms. Naami regularly went to MEK meetings and reported back to Mr. Assadi in cities across Europe, that person said. Though Mr. Saadouni remained his point of contact, Mr. Assadi insisted Ms. Naami accompany him on missions.

Sometimes they would travel to Vienna, meeting Mr. Assadi on a train after multiple transfers to ensure they weren't being followed, people close to the couple said. Mr. Saadouni would debrief Mr. Assadi, receive new orders and leave with bags of cash.

The money allowed the couple to live comfortably. Mr. Saadouni performed odd jobs, and Ms. Naami worked at a clothes ironing service. When the couple became estranged in recent years, they could afford to live separately, with their own apartments and cars.

Earlier this year, Mr. Saadouni paid more than four hundred euros for a ticket to see Roger Waters of Pink Floyd in Antwerp.

Mr. Saadouni believed Mr. Assadi had multiple moles inside MEK, according to a person close to Mr. Saadouni. When grilling him about MEK meetings, Mr. Assadi would

John Bolton, center, at a conference of Iranian dissidents in Villepinte, France, in 2015.
PHOTO: SIAVOSH HOSSEINI/SIPA

show him photos of people he said were there even though Mr. Saadouni hadn't mentioned them, the person said.

Shahin Gobadi, an MEK spokesman, said Mr. Saadouni and Ms. Naami were supporters of the group, though not in its inner circle.

Under orders from Mr. Assadi, the couple became regulars at an annual gathering of Iranian opposition groups organized by MEK outside Paris. Retired U.S. and European officials and ex-politicians with hawkish views on Iran were often invited to speak, including Mr. Giuliani and John Bolton. Now both men are close to Mr. Trump, with Mr. Bolton serving as the national security adviser.

"I'm sure that the Iranians are very alarmed when they see

Giuliani and Bolton and others openly embracing MEK," Mr. Riedel said.

The Iranian regime has also faced widespread protests this year, and blames MEK for helping to stoke them, according to MEK officials.

Days before the June 30 conference, Mr. Assadi summoned Mr. Saadouni and Ms. Naami to Luxembourg.

Mr. Assadi placed a makeup pouch into Ms. Naami's handbag, according to people close to the couple. They said the couple later told investigators Mr. Assadi said the pouch contained a device that was effectively a firecracker, which would make a loud noise but wouldn't hurt anyone.

The Washington Post

August 21, 2018

U.S. court detains Calif. man charged with serving as agent of Iran, surveilling Americans

By Spencer S. Hsu

A California man pleaded not guilty to acting as a covert agent of the government of Iran and was ordered detained Tuesday by a U.S. judge on charges of secretly monitoring a Jewish center in Chicago and American members of an exiled Iranian opposition group.

U.S. Magistrate G. Michael Harvey of the District of Columbia said the case as alleged bore "hallmarks of state action," and held Majid Ghorbani, 59, until trial.

The judge cited the purported use of code names, countersurveillance tactics and "tasking" orders to infiltrate the Mujahideen-e Khalq (MEK), or People's Mujahideen of Iran, a dissident group that seeks regime change in Iran.

Ghorbani, an Iranian citizen and permanent U.S. resident of Costa Mesa, Calif., and co-defendant Ahmadreza Mohammadi Doostdar, 38, a dual U.S.-Iranian citizen, were arrested Aug. 9 and indicted Monday on charges of acting as agents of Iran, violating U.S. sanctions, and conspiracy.

Doostdar is set to appear in federal court Wednesday in Chicago.

Although the men are not charged with espionage, prosecutors told the court they intend to use information obtained under the Foreign Intelligence Surveillance Act, which allows collection of electronic communications overseas. Ghorbani's home and Doostdar's luggage were searched surreptitiously, and U.S. authorities recorded conversations the men conducted on pay phones and in their vehicles.

In a statement Tuesday, the National Council of Resistance of Iran, a Paris-based group linked to the MEK and two of whose members were allegedly targeted by the operation, called the defendants Iranian Intelligence Ministry agents. The group likened the case to those of two people arrested and charged with plotting to bomb an MEK rally in

France in July and two others accused of terrorism against the group in Albania in March.

"The Iranian Resistance once again reiterates the need to prosecute and expel all the regime's Intelligence Ministry and Quds Force agents and all known and undercover agents and mercenaries who pursue the regime's plots in the U.S. and Europe," the group said.

In an hour-long hearing in federal court, Assistant U.S. Attorney Erik Kenerson said that Ghorbani posed a serious risk of flight and that his charges carried a statutory maximum of 35 years in prison if run consecutively.

"The [U.S.] government cannot stop him from going into a consulate, embassy or the Iranian interests section" of the Pakistani Embassy in Washington, nor from obtaining a new Iranian passport and leaving the country, Kenerson said.

"There's no force field that prevents him from doing anything," he added, including continuing to put at risk "U.S. citizens on American soil for exercising their constitutional rights."

According to charging documents, Doostdar entered the United States in about July 2017, allegedly to gather intelligence about targets considered enemies of the Tehran government, and made contact with Ghorbani.

Prosecutors translated Ghorbani's recorded remarks in Farsi as saying he "penetrated" the MEK to send information back to Tehran for "targeting" packages — data the FBI said can be used for the neutralization, arrest, recruitment, or cyber exploitation of a target, as well as "capture/kill operations."

The FBI said Ghorbani named two Washington-based men he surveilled, Alireza Jafarzadeh, deputy director of the NCRI's Washington office and an MEK spokesman, and Ali Safavi, president of the Near East Policy Research consulting firm in

Washington and a member of the NCRI's foreign affairs committee.

Ghorbani's attorney, Assistant Federal Defender Mary Petras, said that Ghorbani's alleged statements were translated and out of context, and she denied that he posed a serious risk of flight. He has lived for 20 years in the United States since immigrating with his parents, sister and brother, lives with his younger brother in Orange County, Calif., and worked as a waiter at the same restaurant for a decade, she said.

Petras noted that Ghorbani's daughter and her fiance were present in the courtroom, traveling from their home in California to support her father.

Prosecutors alleged that Ghorbani was paid $2,000 by Doostdar in late 2017 after turning over photographs of demonstrators at a Sept. 20, 2017, rally in New York City against the Iranian government. An FBI affidavit also said that Ghorbani traveled to Iran to conduct an "in-person briefing" in March and allegedly discussed clandestine methods to provide photos he took of an Iran Freedom Convention for Human Rights in Washington, D.C., on May 4.

Both events were supported by the MEK, which was listed by the U.S. State Department as a terrorist group from 1997 until 2012.

However, Petras said that Ghorbani is accused of taking "photographs of two events" and "two known individuals," containing information that is publicly available on the Internet, including in videos and data "uploaded by MEK itself."

Petras said there is no evidence that Ghorbani traveled to meet with any agent of the Iranian government, as opposed to a possible government supporter, or opponent of MEK.

Appendix

161

August 9, 2018

Iran plots terror on European soil as EU tries to shield regime from Trump sanctions push

By Adam Shaw

As the European Union decries America's restoration of Iran sanctions, the Islamic regime is rewarding Europe's support by ramping up its terror operation on the continent -- allegedly plotting attacks against Iranian dissidents there and politicians who back them.

The Trump administration restored sanctions on the rogue regime this week, a consequence of the U.S. decision to withdraw from the Obama-era Joint Comprehensive Plan of Action (JCPOA). That move provoked a strong response from European leaders, who said they "deeply regret" the U.S. decision.

"The lifting of nuclear-related sanctions is an essential part of the deal," E.U. High Representative Federica Mogherini, along with French, German and British foreign ministers, said in a joint statement, vowing to "protect European economic operators engaged in legitimate business with Iran."

But the regime, while facing significant unrest at home over corruption and mismanagement that has led to water shortages and food price hikes, allegedly has been exporting terror to Europe.

Last month, an Iranian diplomat based in Vienna was one of four arrested for an alleged plot to bomb an annual gathering of Iranian dissident groups in Paris, which Trump lawyer Rudy Giuliani attended.

German prosecutors allege that Assadollah Assadi was a member of the "Ministry of Intelligence and Security," (MOIS) tasked with combating observation groups inside and outside of Iran. He is charged with activity as a foreign agent and conspiracy to commit murder. Iran Foreign Minister Javad Zarif has called the allegations a ploy.

The Wall Street Journal reported that Dutch authorities expelled two Iranian diplomats in July linked to the assassination of one Iranian dissident who was murdered in the Hague in November.

There are also concerns about the regime's presence in Albania, where dissidents told Fox News the Iranian embassy is staffing up and has sent top intelligence operatives. Albania is significant as it was where more than 2,000 Iranian dissidents belonging to People's Mujahedin of Iran (MEK) were relocated from Iraq in 2016.

The National Council of Resistance in Iran (NCRI) said that the regime wanted to murder them in Iraq, and the failure to do so marked a "major setback" for the regime.

Former Albanian Prime Minister Pandeli Majko revealed to Fox News that he has been told by U.S. officials that he needs to increase his security after intelligence of a threat against him.

While he said Iran's strategy in the region is "unprecedented," he also told Fox News, "I am not afraid."

A senior U.S. counterterrorism official confirmed to Fox News that Albanian authorities arrested two Iranian operatives on terror charges earlier this year.

"Iran has a long history over the last 39 years of conducting and planning assassinations and terrorist actions against opponents of the Iranian regime, including a series of assassinations and attack plots in recent years in European countries," the official said.

U.S. officials have not been shy about calling out the terror plots. Secretary of State Mike Pompeo, in a speech last month, pointed to the Paris attempt as proof of the regime's intentions.

"This tells you everything you need to know about the regime: At the same time they're trying to convince Europe to stay in the nuclear deal, they're covertly plotting terrorist attacks in the heart of Europe," he said.

Mohammad Mohaddessin, the chairman of the Foreign Affairs Committee of the National Council of Resistance of Iran (NCRI), said in a statement to Fox News that there is no doubt that the plots are coming from the regime's leadership.

"The Iranian regime's foiled plots in Albania and in Paris were similar to the operations that ISIS carried out in terms of targeting big crowds and inflicting damage to a large number of people at once," he told Fox News in a statement.

"These plots were decided and planned at one body, namely the Supreme National Security Council. These plots were approved by Ali Khamenei, the regime's supreme leader, and were relegated to the MOIS to be carried out."

The alleged terror threats are likely only to increase the pressure on the E.U. to abandon its opposition to sanctions and get on board with U.S. efforts to pressure Iran into either reform or regime change. This week, U.S. Ambassador to the U.N. Nikki Haley accused the bloc of "playing politics" on the issue.

"The E.U. can do what they want but you can't condone the practices that are coming out of Iran, so the E.U. will have a decision to make," Haley told Fox News on Wednesday.

Fox News' Ben Evansky, Rich Edson and The Associated Press contributed to this report.

The New York Times

April 11, 1997

Berlin Court Says Top Iran Leaders Ordered Killings

By Alan Cowell

A court concluded here today that the highest levels of Iran's "political leadership" ordered the September 1992 killing of exiled Iranian Kurdish dissidents in Berlin.

After a three-year trial that included testimony by 166 witnesses, the presiding judge ruled that the killing of four dissidents at the Mykonos restaurant were orchestrated by a secretive "Committee for Special Operations" in Teheran whose members included the country's spiritual leader, the President, the Foreign Minister and high security officials.

The ruling reinforced the Clinton Administration's assertions that Iran's Islamic rulers sponsor terrorism and fueled demands by the United States for Germany and other European allies to end what they call their "critical dialogue" with Iran, a policy that permits flourishing trade with a land that Washington wants ostracized.

While the judge's opinion did not identify the top officials by name, German federal prosecutors during the trial directly accused Ayatollah Ali Khamenei, Iran's spiritual leader, and President Hashemi Rafsanjani of ordering and approving the killings.

"The Iranian political leadership ordered this crime," said the Judge, Frithjof Kubsch. "They made a decision to silence an uncomfortable voice. This is an official liquidation measure ordered without a verdict."

Continue reading the main story

In today's ruling, the most far-reaching judicial condemnation of

Iran's leadership made in Germany, two of the five men accused of involvement in the killing were given life sentences, one was acquitted and two were given jail terms of between 5 and 11 years.

The men were first indicted in May 1993, with prosecutors saying the killings had been the work of Vevak, the Iranian security service, which has been held responsible for a string of killings of exiled political figures and Kurdish dissidents in Paris, Rome, Geneva and Vienna. Until now, however, there has been no case of this magnitude that has implicated highest level of leaders in Iran.

In Washington the State Department's spokesman, Nicholas Burns, immediately seized on the verdict, saying it corroborated America's "long-held view that Iran's sponsorship of terrorism is authorized at senior levels of the Iranian Government."

Mr. Burns also chided the European allies for continuing to maintain ties and trade with Iran. "The 'critical dialogue' has not succeeded in moderating Iran's behavior," he said.

He called on "our European partners" to join the American economic sanctions against Teheran, but added that "the German authorities will now have to draw their own conclusions about how they wish to do business with Iran after this strong and unambiguous verdict."

The German Foreign Ministry said it would not participate "for the foreseeable future" in the policy of "critical dialogue" with Iran -- a

formulation that fell short of suspending the policy altogether.

Mr. Burns said later that he was pleased with that decision, adding, "We hope that the European Union will join the United States in a realistic policy that is aimed at containing Iran and containing its ability to further destabilize the Middle East and to murder its own citizens abroad," he said.

Within hours of the ruling, the German Foreign Ministry said that it was recalling its Ambassador to Teheran and that four Iranian diplomats would be expelled. A Foreign Ministry spokesman also said European officials in Brussels were considering withdrawing their envoys and suspending the "critical dialogue."

Iran, for its part, withdrew its Ambassador in Bonn, Hossein Musavian, and a Foreign Ministry spokesman in Teheran called the ruling "baseless, malicious, one-sided and unfair."

Iranian security forces were deployed at the German Embassy and the German Ambassador's residence in Teheran, apparently to prevent a recurrence of protests.

In The Hague, a spokesman for the European Union said all 15 members of the body had been invited to recall their ambassadors from Teheran. The spokesman, Peter Mollema, also said in a statement that "no progress" could be made in Europe's relationship with Iran "while Iran flouts international norms and indulges in acts of terrorism."

Germany is Iran's biggest trading partner, but Iranian business accounts for only a tiny fraction of Germany's imports and exports, giving Germany huge potential leverage over Iran that Washington maintains should be employed to force political change.

German politicians from both the Government and opposition parties seemed reluctant today to call for an all-out breach in relations with Teheran.

"Breaking off diplomatic relations would be a serious mistake," said Gunter Verheugen, of the opposition Social Democrats. "But it would also be a serious mistake if we carried on as if nothing had happened."

Judge Kubsch said the "Committee for Special Operations" had entrusted Iran's Minister of Intelligence, Ali Fallahiyan, with the killings, in which two heavily armed men loosed a hail of gunfire on a Kurdish opposition leader, Sadiq Sarafkindi, and three colleagues, killing all four. One gunman escaped.

In March, 1996, Germany issued an arrest warrant for Mr. Fallahiyan.

In his ruling today, Judge Kubsch said: "After Fallahiyan reported to the Committee for Special Operations and the committee decided on the liquidation of Dr. Sarafkindi, the panel entrusted him with carrying out the subsequent operations.

"There was no religious background to this act. The reasons, which led to their cruel conclusion, were purely related to the politics of power. The fact that this was ordered by the Government of a state that calls itself a 'state of God' changes nothing. This religious embellishment does not hide the fact that the concern of the ruling regime in Iran was to eliminate opposition beyond its borders."

Iran has denied any involvement in the killings, as did the accused. Mahmud Mohamedi, a Foreign Ministry spokesman in Teheran, said after today's ruling, "We reject these conclusions, which are undocumented and influenced by political campaigns in anti-revolutionary and Zionist circles."

The court today supported prosecution allegations that Kazem Darabi, an Iranian who had worked in Berlin as a grocer, was an Iranian Government agent who planned the attack. The prosecution had also said that Abbas Rhayel, a Lebanese citizen, had been one of two gunmen who shot the Kurdish exiles to death. Both men were given life sentences today.

Two other Lebanese men were sentenced to between 5 and 11 years as accomplices.

The verdict drew wild cheers from hundreds of Iranian exiles who had demonstrated outside the courthouse to demand an end to Germany's relationship with Iran. Iranian Kurds also protested outside the Iranian Embassy in Bonn.

The trial opened on Oct. 28, 1993, three weeks after Mr. Fallahiyan appealed to the authorities to halt it. The hearings took a more dramatic turn in August, 1996, when Abdolhassan Bani Sadr, a former Iranian President, testified that the killings had been ordered by the highest authorities in Teheran.

His information came from conversations involving the allegations of an unidentified Iranian defector, known by German prosecutors as "Source C," who testified at closed hearings in October 1996.

One month later, as the prosecution began a three-day summation,

orchestrated demonstrations broke out in Teheran outside the German Embassy, raising fears for the safety of the 500 German citizens living in Iran.

As today's verdict approached, the Foreign Ministry in Bonn advised Germans not to travel to Iran, despite an assurance by Foreign Minister Ali Akbar Velayati that "we support human values, and German nationals will have full security." The 15 European Union ambassadors were summoned to the Foreign Ministry in Teheran today, Iranian officials said, and were assured of the safety of their citizens.

At the same time, though, Iran has already given a hint of part of its response. Two days ago, the official Iranian news agency reported that 1,000 relatives of Iranians killed in the Iran-Iraq war between 1980 and 1988 would sue 24 German chemical companies accused of helping Iraq acquire chemical weapons.

Scores of Iranian exiles have been threatened, wounded or killed since the Government of Shah Mohammed Reza Pahlevi was overthrown in 1979. The most publicized case is the death sentence leveled against Salman Rushdie, the British author accused of blasphemy in 1989 for his book, "The Satanic Verses."

Several Iranian dissidents have been killed in Europe. In 1991, Shahpur Bakhtiar, the last Prime Minister under the Shah, was found with his throat slit at his villa in France. A French court linked his death to agents for Iran. In 1990 Kazem Rajavi, brother of the leader of an Iranian dissident group, was killed in Switzerland. Others have been killed in Asia and the Middle East.

The New York Times

Sunday, June 25, 1995

U.S. Asserts Iranians Plotted
To Disrupt Rally in Germany

By ELAINE SCIOLINO

Washington, June 24 -- Iranian diplomats working out of their embassy in Bonn plotted to disrupt a huge opposition rally in Germany last week, perhaps with the intention of assassinating a leading Iranian dissident, American intelligence officials said today.

At about the same time, Germany asked two Iranian intelligence officials to leave the country because of evidence that they were planning potentially lethal operations from German territory, the American officials said. The expulsions did not appear to be specifically linked to the plot.

German Foreign Ministry officials denied any knowledge of the plot or the expulsions, although they abruptly banned the opposition leader, Maryam Rajavi, from entering the country to address the rally.

But United States officials said they confirmed the incidents both with German officials and through independent American intelligence-gathering efforts in Germany.

The American disclosure of the incident in Bonn is likely to embarrass the German Government and may further divide the Clinton Administration and its allies in Europe and Asia about how to deal with Iran.

For the United States, evidence of an Iranian-inspired plot in Europe is just more proof that Iran is, as Washington claims, an "outlaw state" that spends hundreds of millions of dollars a year on terrorism and has embarked on a "crash" course to develop nuclear weapons. The evidence is certain to be seized on by the Administration to bolster its uncompromising though much-criticized campaign to undermine the Teheran Government through economic means.

Both American and German intelligence concluded last year that Iran is using its embassy in Bonn as an informal headquarters of the Iranian intelligence services in Europe, and as a base from which to watch its 100,000 citizens in

Germany and to buy militarily useful technology and equipment.

The German determination to remain silent about the plot and expulsion underscores the vast difference in approach between the United States and Iran's major trading partners, which have refused to join the American economic embargo. They argue that the best means of changing Iran's behavior is to embrace it, rather than isolate it.

President Clinton acknowledged that difference in a news conference earlier this month when he said, "I don't know that we're on the same wave length" with the allies, adding, "the evidence is that constructive engagement with the Iranians has, at least so far, failed to produce any positive results."

Most of the allies would agree with the American case -- despite official denials in Teheran -- that Iran is positioning itself to become a nuclear power, building its arsenal of chemical weapons and ballistic missiles, undermining Middle East peace efforts, and supporting terrorist groups and acts worldwide.

But the Europeans and the Japanese contend that the United States, with its relentless name-calling and sweeping charges often without concrete proof, has tended to distort the Iranian threat for domestic political reasons, including a desire to neutralize an anti-Iranian Congress. There is also a strong perception abroad that the anti-Iranian stance of the United States reflects the increased influence of Israel in shaping American perceptions of Iran, at a time when Iran is strongly supporting terrorist groups determined to undermine Middle East peace talks.

Iran has done little to help the Europeans and Japanese justify their conciliatory approach, as shown most recently by Teheran's rejection on Thursday of an appeal from the 15 European Union nations to lift the death threat imposed against the novelist Salman Rushdie.

Early last week, when the German Government abruptly banned Mrs. Rajavi, the Iranian opposition leader, from entering Germany, officials explained that as the head of a movement determined to violently overthrow the Government of another country, she was not welcome.

But American intelligence officials concluded that there was another reason as well: the discovery by German intelligence that Iran's embassy in Bonn was assembling a team from the terrorist group the Party of God to violently disrupt the rally, and perhaps assassinate Mrs. Rajavi.

Since Germany has led the Europeans in defending what it calls a "critical dialogue" with Teheran that is based on high-level exchanges and efforts to boost trade, it is not surprising that German authorities have kept quiet about the alleged plot, but have clung to the official line.

"We cannot allow cause for the violent overthrow of a government from our own territory," said Sabine Sparwasser, a Foreign Ministry spokesman in Bonn. Asked whether Germany has asked for the expulsion of two Iranian diplomats, she added, "To my knowledge there have been no recent cases where we told Iranians from the embassy to leave."

Officials in the office of Bernd Schmidbauer, the intelligence coordinator for Chancellor Helmut Kohl and the senior German official involved in contacts with Iran, declined comment on any matter involving Iran. It was Mr. Schmidbauer who infuriated the Clinton Adminstration after he allowed Ali Fallahian, the head of Iran's intelligence services, to visit Germany in 1993, and tour intelligence headquarters in Wiesbaden.

Of all the arguments the Administration has made against Iran, its case that Iran supports terrorism has been the most difficult to make. That is because American officials say they are reluctant to disclose information that could reveal intelligence sources and methods in gathering the information and thus compromise the operations involved.

The Washington Post

November 21, 1993

Killing Of Iranian Dissenters: 'Bloody Trail Back To Tehran'

By Rick Atkinson
Washington Post Staff Writer

BERLIN -- On a chilly September night last year, two masked gunmen burst into the back room of the Mykonos restaurant here and, in a bloody scene repeated again and again during the last decade, opened fire on expatriate opponents of Iran's fundamentalist Islamic regime.

This time the targets were a Kurdish separatist leader and three of his top aides. As in dozens of similar murders, investigators found few clues except for four bullet-riddled bodies sprawled amid the overturned tables and shattered cups.

Yet, unlike nearly all of the previous assassinations in France, Switzerland, Italy, Turkey, and at least eight other countries, this time alleged killers soon were caught. Five defendants, including an Iranian accused of being an agent of Tehran's Ministry of Intelligence and Security, known in Persian as VEVAK, are now on trial in Berlin.

Extraordinary security measures include defendants' docks encased in bulletproof glass, double searches of all lawyers and spectators, and an anti-grenade net draped at the court entrance.

The Mykonos murders have refocused public attention in Europe on the systematic extermination of Iran's political foes, as well as the West's relations with Tehran. The investigation and trial have provided new insights into the operation of meticulously organized death squads directly linked to the rule of Iranian President Ali Akbar Hashemi Rafsanjani, according to U.S. and German officials.

The bold brutality of such killings has triggered protests from human rights groups and Western governments. Amnesty International issued a report

last week documenting and condemning the murder of Iranian dissidents abroad. "We're seeing a growing pattern of killings and this bloody trail leads back to Tehran," James O'Dea, Washington director of the organization, said in an interview.

Sweden ordered the expulsion of three Iranian diplomats on Monday for spying on Iranian expatriates; Tehran retaliated on Wednesday by kicking out three Swedish diplomats. The State Department has declared Iran to be the most active of all state sponsors of terrorism. It alleges that Iranian agents or surrogate groups carried out more than 20 attacks in 1992 alone.

Leery of Provoking Iran

Despite such recent measures, the West's response to Tehran's alleged complicity has often been tepid or inconsistent. Commercial interests and desires to avoid provoking Iran sometimes have caused Western governments to soft-pedal their criticisms, U.S. and European officials say.

Germany's Federal Criminal Office noted that although "Iran does not shrink from committing serious crimes in pursuing its opponents," the "reaction in the West is most likely to be verbal."

Germany, which sold more than $5 billion in goods and services to Iran last year, is a case in point. In early October, three weeks before the Mykonos trial opened, Chancellor Helmut Kohl's top intelligence adviser, Bernd Schmidbauer, met in Bonn with Ali Fallahian, Iran's intelligence minister. Fallahian, whom the German press has dubbed "the sixth defendant" in the Mykonos murders, is suspected by

prosecutors of being the mastermind of the attack.

But when investigators suggested filing charges against Fallahian during his visit, Bonn insisted that the Iranian was a "state guest" who was not to be harassed, according to state prosecutor Bruno Jobst.

Schmidbauer has defended his talks with Fallahian by suggesting that Germany is trying to mediate between Tehran and Western countries that prefer to isolate Iran as an international outlaw. "If you don't cooperate internationally," he told the German newspaper Die Welt, "you get crimes on your own soil."

The Iranian government has denied any connection to attacks. A spokesman for the embassy in Bonn reiterated those denials, adding that allegations of complicity in the Mykonos case "are absolutely baseless. . . . We also want to find out who's behind the murder."

German law enforcement officials say, however, that the six judges presiding over the Mykonos trial will find ample evidence of Iranian government involvement. They note that on Aug. 30, 1992, Fallahian told an Iranian television interviewer, "We track them {opposition groups} outside the country, too. We have them under surveillance. . . . Last year, we succeeded in striking fundamental blows to their top members."

Iranian in the Dock

Less than three weeks later, another blow was struck with the four Mykonos murders. Of the five men arrested -- one questioned shortly after the shootings confessed and implicated the others -- four are Lebanese with links to

Appendix

167

Hezbollah, the pro-Iranian extremist group. The fifth man is Kazem Darabi, 34, an Iranian vegetable vendor who moved to Germany 13 years ago and has been convicted previously of attacking Iranian dissidents.

The indictment charges that Darabi "was an agent of the Iranian secret service VEVAK and a member of the Iranian Revolutionary Guard with close ties to Hezbollah in Lebanon." The indictment contends that Darabi "received from VEVAK the secret service's order to liquidate" the leader of the Kurdistan Democratic Party of Iran (PDKI) while he was in Berlin for a conference.

Although not in the Mykonos restaurant when the killings occurred on Sept. 17, 1992, Darabi allegedly recruited the assassins, organized the plot, provided the weapons and orchestrated the escape. The Berlin attack "is the consequence of countermeasures against the Iranian opposition, particularly the PDKI, as personally described by the secret service minister" Fallahian, the German Federal Office for the Protection of the Constitution asserted in a report that formed the basis of the indictment.

The Berlin murders are only a recent example of what intelligence and law enforcement officials say is a campaign that has not diminished since the death of Ayatollah Ruhollah Khomeini in 1989 and Rafsanjani's accession. "Behind all these crimes stands a sovereign state with all of its logistical capabilities," the German Federal Criminal Office report asserted.

An Iranian resistance movement, the People's Mojahedin, contends the Tehran regime has killed 100,000 opponents in Iran and tortured another 150,000. The organization, which is unrelated to the anti-communist Afghan guerrillas called mujaheddin, lists nearly 100 assassinations of or assaults on Iranian expatriates since the fundamentalist regime took power in 1979. Western law enforcement officials have found links to Tehran in many of these cases. Among them:

On March 16, Mohammed Hussein Naghdi, a leading dissident with the National Council of Resistance of Iran, was shot in the face and killed while sitting in his car in downtown Rome. The two assassins escaped on a motorcycle through midday traffic. The

Italian interior minister subsequently described the murder as "part of an extremely dangerous strategy {by Islamic fundamentalists} aimed at subverting Europe and the West."

In Turkey, approximately 50 Iranian dissidents have been killed, as well as secular Turks who spoke out against Iranian fundamentalism. Among the attacks was the kidnapping in Istanbul on June 4, 1992, of Mansour Amini, a member of the People's Mojahedin. His body, with its fingernails pulled out and genitals mutilated, was found in a shallow grave. Nineteen Turkish fundamentalists eventually charged with Amini's murder and two other killings had "clear connections to Iran," according to Turkey's interior minister.

Abdul Rahman Qassemlou, leader of the Kurdistan Democratic Party of Iran, and two associates were shot to death in Vienna in 1989, after being lured to a meeting with representatives from the Tehran government. An arrest warrant was issued for two Iranian gunmen and the Austrian foreign minister said it was "probable" that Iran was behind the killings. Qassemlou's successor, Sadeq Sharafkandi, was the primary target in the Berlin killings three years later.

Former prime minister Shapour Bakhtiar, 76, had his throat slit and his secretary was stabbed to death outside Paris on Aug. 6, 1991. An investigating French magistrate uncovered an extensive terror network that helped the assassins carry out the murder and escape from France using forged passports. Several arrests have been made in the case and warrants issued for two Iranians. U.S. intelligence officials have termed it unlikely that such a high-level assassination would have been undertaken without Rafsanjani's approval.

Another Iranian dissident and close associate of Bakhtiar, Abdel Rahman Boroumand, was stabbed to death in Paris in April 1991. The former prime minister had eluded an earlier attempt on his life in 1980, when men posing as journalists killed a French policeman and a neighbor in a shootout at Bakhtiar's house. The convicted leader, a pro-Iranian Lebanese, was released in 1990 in a swap for French hostages in Lebanon.

The Norwegian publisher of Salman Rushdie's "The Satanic Verses" was wounded by three bullets outside his

Oslo home in mid-October. Rushdie, a British author accused of blasphemy by Khomeini, has been in hiding since 1989, when Tehran issued a death warrant and put a $2 million bounty on his head. The Japanese translator of "The Satanic Verses" was murdered and an Italian translator escaped an assassination attempt in 1991.

Other Iranian dissidents killed in recent years include Bahman Javadi, shot by a gunman using a silencer-equipped pistol on Cyprus in 1989; Ataellah Bayahmadi, a former colonel in intelligence, shot in his hotel room in Dubai in June 1989; and Majid-Reza Ibrahimi, a Mojahedin member shot while shopping in Baghdad last month.

Swiss Collect Evidence

Perhaps the case that offers the clearest link to Tehran was the murder in Switzerland on Aug. 24, 1990, of Kazem Rajavi, head of the Mojahedin organization in Geneva. While driving home from a tobacco shop, Rajavi was ambushed by gunmen in two cars. After pinning Rajavi's red Datsun against the curb, one assassin opened fire with an Uzi 9mm submachine gun. Six bullets hit Rajavi.

Swiss police and magistrate Roland Chatelain subsequently implicated 13 Iranians in the plot. Most had entered Switzerland with diplomatic passports issued in Tehran on the same date with the notation "on assignment." Most also had arrived on Iran Air's Tehran-to-Geneva flights over several months preceding the murder, using tickets with consecutive serial numbers, according to Chatelain's report. Several of the men flew from Geneva to Vienna less than two hours after the killing.

The accumulated evidence, Chatelain declared, "permits confirmation of a direct involvement by one or more official Iranian services."

Some observers charge that the West's efforts to counter the murder spree ring hollow. "Given the seriousness of a government sending its agents out to kill opposition leaders, the response has been inadequate," said O'Dea, Amnesty's Washington director. "There is routine torture, routine levels of repression. And because the pattern is repeated, governments have accepted that it is now the norm for Iran."

The Washington Post

Thursday, July 19, 1990

Lawmakers Rebuke Iran For Policy of Terrorism

By George Lardner Jr.
Washington Post Staff Write

One hundred sixty-two House members assailed the Iranian government this week, saying the April assassination of an opposition leader in Switzerland proves terrorism is still an "indispensable pillar" of Tehran's foreign policy.

The accusations were in a letter sponsored by Rep. Mervyn M. Dymally (D-Calif.), and sent Tuesday to Massoud Rajavi, head of the Iraq-based National Council of Resistance and his organization, the People's Mojahedin.

His brother, Kazem Rajavi, 56, was gunned down April 24, authorities said, by a four-man assassination squad that stopped his car near his home in a Geneva suburb where he was a Mojahedin human rights lobbyist.

Swiss investigating magistrates recently reported that "one or more official Iranian agencies were directly involved in the assassination." They said there was evidence that 13 persons, all with Iranian government service passports, played roles in the "minutely planned" killing.

Dymally, chairman of the House Foreign Affairs subcommittee on international operations, said 99 Democrats and 62 Republicans signed his letter, which voiced support for the resistance's "peaceful and democratic aims."

A spokesman for the Iranian United Nations Mission in New York, Ramin Rafi, denounced the letter, calling the signers "tools of a terrorist organization."

Dymally's press secretary, Marwan Burgan, refused to disclose those who signed. Dymally did not return phone calls.

Iranian officials have denied involvement in the Rajavi assassination. Rafi blamed it on Mojahedin "internal differences."

Opposition leaders have charged that Iranian officials in Geneva were infuriated by Kazem Rajavi's effectiveness in discrediting a report last February on the human rights situation in Iran by Galindo Pohl, a U.N. investigator.

The slain man's widow, Michelle Rajavi, said she is convinced the mildly worded report by Pohl, a Salvadoran lawyer who visited Iran last winter for the U.N. Human Rights Commission in Geneva, cleared the way for her husband's assassination.

Swiss police said some of the passports of the 13 implicated in the killing were issued in Tehran on the same date and that most of the individuals flew to Switzerland together from Tehran, using consecutively numbered tickets. Several, police said, flew to Vienna right after the shooting.

Rajavi's widow and another brother-in-law, Paris cardiologist Saleh Rajavi, visited the United States this month to denounce what they call Tehran's "terrorist-diplomat" network in Europe, centered in Geneva.

The widow said she fled Switzerland last month because of harassment from unidentified Iranians.

The visiting Rajavis also protested a planned new U.N. human rights evaluation of Iran this summer by Pohl, whose earlier report was called a whitewash by critics in Congress and Europe.

His February report dismissed as "speculation" reports of political prisoners' executions on trumped-up drug charges. Pohl said Iran had held no public executions for five months, despite numerous accounts in government-owned newspapers of public beheadings and hangings.

Dymally's letter pointed out that the State Department's last annual global terrorism report brands Iran "the most active state sponsor" of terrorism in 1989, having backed 28 terrorist incidents and assassinations of "at least five Iranian dissidents" during the year.

Rafi said Iran has "already rejected" the report.

Officials at State, while defending Pohl, agreed this month that his report, based heavily on statements and witnesses supplied by the Tehran regime, was "not an accurate reflection" of Iran's human rights situation, and they expressed hope that the regime would be more "forthcoming" on his next visit.

The Washington Post

Friday, April 27, 1990

Iranian Exiles Accuse Rafsanjani of Directing Terrorism, Killings Abroad

By George Lardner Jr.
Washington Post Staff Write

Iranian exiles yesterday accused Iranian President Ali Akbar Hashemi Rafsanjani of secretly directing a continuing campaign of terrorism and assassinations abroad while striving for a moderate image by promoting the release of foreign hostages.

Spokesmen for the People's Mojaheddin, a leading opposition movement, charged at a news conference here that Iranian diplomats close to Rafsanjani were responsible for the killing in Switzerland this week of Kazem Rajavi, a prominent opponent of the fundamentalist government in Tehran.

Rajavi, 56, was killed Tuesday morning in a hail of gunfire, apparently from an automatic weapon, as he was driving toward his home outside Geneva. He was shot in the head at close range by one of two men in a car that blocked his auto, police said. He was the brother of Massoud Rajavi, leader of the Iraq-based Mojaheddin.

It was the second shooting in recent weeks of an Iranian dissident abroad. On March 14, gunmen in Turkey attacked the car of Hossein Mir-Abedini, another senior Mojaheddin member, as he was on his way to Istanbul Airport. He was shot in the abdomen.

Alireza Jafarzadeh, a Mojaheddin spokesman here, said his group had a tape of a telephone call from the Iranian consul general in Geneva, Karim-Abadi, to Tehran after the Rajavi assassination, saying that "everything had gone right" and that "the persons are back in the consulate." He said the cassette was turned over to Swiss authorities.

Opposition spokesmen here and abroad charged that Siroos Nasseri, Iran's ambassador to the United Nations in Geneva, told Rajavi in late Februry, in the presence of witnesses, that he would be liquidated.

Iran's U.N. Mission in Geneva denied any involvement in the murder and called the accusation "a mere lie."

According to Jafarzadeh, Nasseri, a Rafsanjani "protege," was furious at Rajavi for being so effective in discrediting a report by a U.N. human rights investigator in late February that there had been no public executions in Iran for five months. Newspapers and radio broadcasts in Iran reported repeatedly in January and February on public hangings and beheadings.

Jafarzadeh charged that Nasseri coordinated the assassination with the help of Karim-Abadi and the Iranian ambassador to Switzerland, Mohamed-Hossein Malaek, a former student leader who took part in the 1979 seizure of the U.S. Embassy in Tehran and in subsequent interrogations of American hostages.

The resistance spokesman, citing "sources" inside Iran, also asserted that "Rafsanjani was directly monitoring this whole process throughout the course of the operation {against Rajavi} and after that."

"While Rafsanjani is with one hand cutting deals with the West, with the other he is busy carrying out assassinations, tortures and executions," Jafarzadeh said. He denounced talk that Iranian-sponsored terrorism is the work of a "so-called radical" faction and called Rafsanjani's image as a moderate "a ridiculous fable."

"Terrorism is the very cornerstone of this regime," Jafarzadeh said.

Switzerland's governing Federal Council condemned Rajavi's killing and promised a vigorous investigation. Rajavi's "followers and friends feel hurt," said Swiss Embassy spokesman Jean-Jacques De Dardel. "Swiss public order has also been attacked. We just don't tolerate assassinations on our soil."

Rajavi had asked Swiss authorities for police protection in a Dec. 21, 1987, letter, saying it had become "indispensable."

"Unfortunately, not enough sensitivity was shown to this case," Jafarzadeh said.

Endnotes

1   ISNA News Agency, August 28, 2018 (Translated from Farsi) https://bit.ly/2TXdQTP

2   Recent damage inflicted on Iran by U.S. will gain a response, January 9, 2018 http://english.khamenei.ir/news/5394/Recent-damage-inflicted-on-Iran-by-U-S-will-gain-a-response

3   Rouhani calls on Macron to act over anti-Iran 'terrorists' in France, January 2, 2018, https://www.dailymail.co.uk/wires/afp/article-5229589/Rouhani-calls-Macron-act-anti-Iran-terrorists-France.html

4   Iran plots terror on European soil as EU tries to shield regime from Trump sanctions push, Fox News, August 9, 2018, Adam Shaw, http:// www.foxnews.com/politics/2018/08/09/iran-plots-terror-on-european-soil-as-eu-triesto-shield-regime-from-trump-sanctions-push.html

5   Iran: Select Europe-Based Operational Activity, 1979-2018, Fact sheet of the U.S. Department of State on the Iranian terrorism in Europe, complied by the National Counterterrorsim Center, July 5, 2018, https://www.state.gov/j/ct/rls/other/283789.htm.

6   Interview of Edi Rama, Prime Minister of Albania, Vizion Plus Tv, April 19, 2018.

7   Ibid, Fox news

8   Albania expels two Iranian diplomats for harming national security, December 20, 2018 https://english.alarabiya.net/en/News/world/2018/12/20/Albania-expels-two-Iranian-diplomats-for-harming-national-security.html

9   Secretary Pompeo's Call With Albanian Foreign Minister Ditmir Bushati, December 21, 2018 https://www.state.gov/r/pa/prs/ps/2018/12/288252.htm

10   Amb. John Bolton's Tweet, December 19, 2018 https://
     twitter.com/AmbJohnBolton/status/1075494980922298370

11   U.S. Embassy in Tirana website; https://al.usembassy.gov/
     u-s-embassy-statement-25/

12   Bags of Cash and a Bomb Plot: Inside a Covert Iranian
     Operation in Europe, October 31, 2018, https://www.wsj.
     com/articles/bags-of-cash-and-a-bomb-plot-inside-a-
     covert-iranian-operation-in-europe-1540978201

13   Foiled Paris bomb plot raises fears that Iran is planning
     attacks in Europe, October 12, 2018, https://www.
     washingtonpost.com/world/national-security/foiled-
     paris-bomb-plot-raises-fears-that-iran-is-planning-
     attacks-in-europe/2018/10/11/2ccf8d0a-c8b9-11e8-b1ed-
     1d2d65b86d0c_story.html

14   Bags of Cash and a Bomb Plot: Inside a Covert Iranian
     Operation in Europe, October 31, 2018, https://www.wsj.
     com/articles/bags-of-cash-and-a-bomb-plot-inside-a-
     covert-iranian-operation-in-europe-1540978201

15   Iranian diplomat suspected of plotting attack in France, July
     11, 2018, https://www.cbsnews.com/news/iranian-diplomat-
     assadollah-assadi-suspected-of-plotting-attack-in-france/

16   "Iran Plotted To Bomb A Meeting Near Paris That Former
     US Officials Attended, Germany Says," Buzzfeed News, July
     11, 2018, Mitch Prothero, https://www.buzzfeednews.com/
     article/mitchprothero/germany-has-charged-aniranian-
     diplomat-with-plotting-to

17   Reuters, October 26.

18   France Freezes Iranian Assets Over Bomb Plot Blamed on
     Tehran, October 2, 2018, https://www.wsj.com/articles/
     france-freezes-iranian-assets-over-bomb-plot-blamed-on-
     tehran-1538487926

19   Agence France Presse, France accuses Iran over bomb plot
     near Paris, October 3, 2018, https://www.thejakartapost.
     com/news/2018/10/03/france-accuses-iran-over-bomb-
     plot-near-paris.html

20   France points finger at Iran over bomb plot, seizes assets, Oct 2, 2018, https://www.reuters.com/article/us-france-security/france-points-finger-at-iran-over-bomb-plot-seizes-assets-idUSKCN1MC12X

21   Extradition of Iranian Official Asadollah Assadi for Role in Paris Terrorist Plot, October 10, 2018, https://www.state.gov/secretary/remarks/2018/10/286532.htm

22   France Ties Iran to Bomb Plot, and Freezes Spy Agency Assets, October 2, 2018, https://www.nytimes.com/2018/10/02/world/europe/france-iran-spy-bombing.html

23   https://www.congress.gov/bill/115th-congress/house-resolution/1034/text

24   https://www.congress.gov/congressional-record/2018/7/11/extensions-of-remarks-section/article/e997-2

25   https://www.apnews.com/fe1d8169e8ea45bfb46fef07f53e8a61

26   Ibid

27   https://www.state.gov/documents/organization/286410.pdf

28   https://www.nbcnews.com/news/world/alleged-iranian-bomb-plot-france-wake-call-europe-u-s-n915986

29   Ibid

30   http://www.thetower.org/6741-pompeo-paris-bombing-plot-lay-bare-irans-continued-support-for-terror/

31   Two Individuals Charged For Acting as Illegal Agents of the Government of Iran, Release by the Department of Justice, August 20, 2018, https:// www.justice.gov/usao-dc/pr/two-individuals-charged-acting-illegal-agentsgovernment-iran

32   Ibid

33   U.S. court detains Calif. man charged with serving as agent of Iran, surveilling Americans, August 21, 2018, https://www.washingtonpost.com/local/public-safety/us-

charges-two-men-with-serving-as-agents-of-iran-spying-on-americans-and-jewish-center/2018/08/20/e6d69252-a4bf-11e8-8fac-12e98c13528d_story.html

34 Two Individuals Charged For Acting as Illegal Agents of the Government of Iran, August 20, 2018, https://www.justice.gov/usao-dc/pr/two-individuals-charged-acting-illegal-agents-government-iran

35 ibid

36 U.S. court detains Calif. man charged with serving as agent of Iran, surveilling Americans, August 21, 2018, https://www.washingtonpost.com/local/public-safety/us-charges-two-men-with-serving-as-agents-of-iran-spying-on-americans-and-jewish-center/2018/08/20/e6d69252-a4bf-11e8-8fac-12e98c13528d_story.html

37 United States of America vs. Majig Ghorbani and Ahmadreza Mohammadi-Doostdar, August 8, 2018, available on the Department of Justice website, https://www.justice.gov/ usao-dc/press-release/file/1088526/download and https://www.justice.gov/ usao-dc/press-release/file/1088531/download

38 Riechmann, Deb, "2 alleged agents of Iran arrested for spying in US," The Associated Press, August 25, 2018, https://www.usnews.com/news/best-states/washington-dc/articles/2018-08-22/2-alleged-agents-of-iran-arrested-for-spying-in-us

39 California man accused of working as an agent of Iran, August 21, 2018, https://www.mercurynews.com/2018/08/21/costa-mesa-man-accused-of-working-as-an-agent-of-iran/

40 https://twitter.com/SenRubioPress/status/1032012264541483008

41 'Denmark shuts links to Sweden and Germany as police hunt car,' Reuters, September 28, 2018, https://in.reuters.com/article/denmark-security/denmark-shuts-links-to-sweden-and-germany-as-police-hunt-car-idINKCN1M81PU

42 http://www.mynewsdesk.com/dk/koebenhavns-politi/
    pressreleases/koebenhavns-politi-efterlyser-bil-2724905

43 Denmark shuts bridge to Sweden and Germany as police
    hunt car involved in 'kidnapping', Metro, September 28,
    2018, https://metro.co.uk/2018/09/28/denmark-shuts-
    bridge-to-sweden-and-germany-as-police-hunt-car-
    involved-in-kidnapping-amp-7988185/

44 'Iranian spy service suspected of assassination plot in
    Denmark: security chief,' Reuters, October 30, 2018,
    https://www.reuters.com/article/us-denmark-security/
    iranian-spy-service-suspected-of-assassination-plot-in-
    denmark-security-chief-idUSKCN1N41N4

45 'Swedish police seize suspected Iranian spy over murder
    plot,' The Local, October 20, 2018, https://www.thelocal.
    se/20181030/swedish-intelligence-seizes-suspected-
    iranian-spy-after-murder-plot

46 'Samuelsen to Iran: Planned assassination on Danish
    soil completely unacceptable,' Statement by Denmark's
    Ministry of Foreign Affairs, October 30, 2018, https://bit.
    ly/2I0gx5x

47 ibid

48 statement by Foreign Minister Samuelsen on illegal Iranian
    intelligence activities in Denmark, Denmark's Ministry of
    Foreign Affairs, October 31, 2018
    http://um.dk/en/news/
    newsdisplaypage/?newsid=81e3e573-6f80-4bbe-910e-
    0d838fb1b6a1

49 'Iranian spy service suspected of assassination plot in
    Denmark: security chief,' Reuters, October 30, 2018,
    https://www.reuters.com/article/us-denmark-security/
    iranian-intelligence-service-suspected-of-attempted-attack-
    in-denmark-security-chief-idUSKCN1N41N4

50 Copenhagen accuses Iran of planning to kill opponent on
    Danish soil, October 30, 2018, https://politi.co/2G2OHUa

51 'EU open to Iran sanctions after foiled France, Denmark
    plots: diplomats,' Reuters, November 19, 2018,

https://www.reuters.com/article/us-iran-nuclear-eu/eu-open-to-iran-sanctions-after-foiled-france-denmark-plots-diplomats-idUSKCN1NO1OQ

52 'Swedish police seize suspected Iranian spy over murder plot,' The Local, October 30, 2018, https://www.thelocal.se/20181030/swedish-intelligence-seizes-suspected-iranian-spy-after-murder-plot

53 'Norwegian-Iranian at the Embassy in March,' Norway Today, November 8, 2018, http://norwaytoday.info/news/norwegian-iranian-celebrated-with-the-ambassador/

54 'Norway minister resigns after breaching security rules during Iran trip,' Reuters, August 13, 2018, https://www.reuters.com/article/us-norway-minister-iran/norway-minister-resigns-after-breaching-security-rules-during-iran-trip-idUSKBN1KY19M

55 'PST investigates minister's partner,' NewsinEnglish.no, August 10, 2018 https://www.newsinenglish.no/2018/08/10/pst-investigates-ministers-partner/

56 Tricks of Iran Regime's Intelligence, Records of the Arrested Agent in Denmark, 11/11/2018, https://bit.ly/2QwDluh

57 ibid

58 Albania expels Iranian diplomats on national security grounds, December 19, 2018, https://www.reuters.com/article/us-albania-iran-expulsion/albania-expels-iranian-diplomats-on-national-security-grounds-idUSKCN1OI2R7

59 Albania expels Iran envoy in 'terrorist' row, December 20, 2018, https://www.bbc.com/news/world-europe-46632612

60 Iran diplomats expelled from Albania plotted against dissidents, source says https://www.independent.co.uk/news/world/europe/iran-albania-diplomats-dissidents-mek-terrorism-trump-bolton-irgc-a8692876.html

61 In shift, EU sanctions Iran over planned Europe attacks https://www.reuters.com/article/us-iran-sanctions/in-shift-eu-sanctions-iran-over-planned-europe-attacks-idUSKCN1P20UA

62   Iran says it will reciprocate after EU sanctions Iranians
      https://www.reuters.com/article/us-iran-sanctions-eu/
      iran-says-it-will-reciprocate-after-eu-sanctions-iranians-
      idUSKCN1P31NZ

63   State-run Ressalat daily, July 20, 1987

64   "The Tehran Connection", Time Magazine, March 21, 1994,
      Thomas Sancton, http://content.time.com/time/magazine/
      article/0,9171,164031,00.html

65   "Iran's Ministry of Intelligence and Security: A Profile," A
      report prepared by the Federal Research Division, Library
      of Congress, under an interagency agreement with the
      Combatting Terrorism Technical Support Office's Irregular
      Warfare Support Program, December 2012, page 13

66   ibid, page 29

67   Edgar O'Ballance, in "Islamic Fundamentalist Terrorism,
      1979-1995, The Iranian Connection."
      http://www.worldcat.org/title/islamic-fundamentalist-
      terrorism-1979-95-the-iranian-connection/oclc/34471538

68   "The Armed Forces of the Islamic Republic of Iran: An
      Assessment", Middle East Review of International Affairs,
      March 2, 2001. http://www.rubincenter.org/2001/03/
      eisenstadt-2001-03-02/

69   Book of verdicts of Mykonos trial.

70   http://i2.cdn.turner.com/cnn/2011/images/10/11/
      complaint.amended.pdf

71   Washington Post, May 30, 2013 https://www.
      washingtonpost.com/world/national-security/
      man-in-iran-backed-plot-to-kill-saudi-ambassador-
      gets-25-years/2013/05/30/0435e7a2-c952-11e2-8da7-
      d274bc611a47_story.html

72   Mullahs' intelligence dispatches agent to Albania as
      refugee to disrupt transfer of Camp Liberty residents,
      December 2, 2013, https://www.ncr-iran.org/en/ncri-
      statements/terrorism-fundamentalism/15404-mullahs-

intelligence-dispatches-agent-to-albania-as-refugee-to-disrupt-transfer-of-camp-liberty-residents

73   Iran's Ministry of Intelligence and Security: A Profile, December 2012, https://fas.org/irp/world/iran/mois-loc.pdf

74   Statement of the Office of German Federal Prosecutor, July 11, 2018

75   Opcit, report prepared by the Federal Research Division, Library of Congress

76   "Killing of Iranian dissenters: Bloody trail back to Tehran", Washington Post, November 21, 1993, Rick Atkinson, https://www.washingtonpost.com/archive/politics/1993/11/21/killing-of-iranian-dissenters-bloody-trail-back-to-tehran/0a28474b-9ab1-485f-9949-fc18882fa909

77   "The Tehran Connection", Time Magazine, March 21, 1994, Thomas Sancton, http://content.time.com/time/magazine/article/0,9171,164031,00.html

78   Eskort Nach Teheran, Peter Pilz, Wien, 1997.

79   Ibid

80   http://www.refworld.org/docid/3ae6a8170.html

81   "Tale of Deadly Iranian Network Woven in Paris : Terrorism: An assassination trial's threads lead as far as California, uncovering a wealth of spy data along the way", Los Angeles Times, November 3, 1994, William Rempel

82   "Suspect in Bakhtiar assassination eludes police", Washington Post, August 17, 1991, Sharon Waxman, https://www.washingtonpost.com/archive/politics/1991/08/17/suspects-in-bakhtiar-assassination-elude-police/3e63ddd8-9c96-44c6-80c7-44840d9c9f58/?utm_term=.7e7ad56f923e

83   "Iranian assassin released from French prison amid 'deal' claims," Daily Telegraph, May 19, 2010, https://www.telegraph.co.uk/news/worldnews/europe/france/7738360/Iranian-assassin-released-from-French-prison-amid-deal-claims.html

84 "France convicts 2 Iranians in Murder of Exiled Leader: Courts: Prosecutor says Tehran at the heart of group that stabbed former prime minister of Iran", Los Angeles Times, December 7, 1994, Scott Kraft, http://articles.latimes.com/1994-12-07/news/mn-5958_1_iranian-government

85 Iran Ronen, "Secret War with Iran," 2008

86 Annual report of Bundesamt fur Verfassungsschutz (BVF) or Federal Office for the Protection of the Constitution of Germany. 1999.

87 The report by the Office of the Protection of the Constitution- North Rhine Westphalia, Germany for the year 2017, published in July 2018.

88 "By the Ayatollah's Decree," The New York Times, September 16, 2011, Caroline Moorehead, https://www.nytimes.com/2011/09/18/books/review/assassins-of-the-turquoise-palace-by-roya-hakakian-book-review.html

89 "Berlin Court says top Iran leaders ordered killings," The New York Times, April 11, 1997, Alan Cowell, https://www.nytimes.com/1997/04/11/world/berlin-court-says-top-iran-leaders-ordered-killings.html

90 "The Assassins' Trail: Unraveling the Mykonos Killings", World Affairs Journal, November/December 2011, Marcus Wilford, http://www.worldaffairsjournal.org/article/assassins%E2%80%99-trail-unraveling-mykonos-killings

91 "U.S. Asserts Iranians Plotted To Disrupt Rally in Germany," The New York Times, June 25, 1995, Elaine Sciolino, https://www.nytimes.com/1995/06/25/world/us-asserts-iranians-plotted-to-disrupt-rally-in-germany.html

92 "Tarha va Toutehahaye Vezarat Ettelat alyeh Mojahedin. Namehe va asnad Jamshid Tafrashi" (Plots and plans of the MOIS against the PMOI/MEK, the letters and documents of Jamshid Tafrashi), Committee of security and Counter-terrorism of the National Council of Resistance of Iran, winter of 2001, page 92

93 The New York Times, June 25, 1995

94   "Germany Charges two Iranians with spying on opposition members", Associated Press, April 8, 2016 http://www.dailymail.co.uk/wires/ap/article-3530019/Germany-charges-2-Iranians-spying-opposition-members.html

95   https://www.seattletimes.com/nation-world/germany-arrests-pakistani-accused-of-spying-for-iran/

96   "German Trial Reveals Details of Spy Case Authorities Link to Iran", Wall Street Journal, April 12, 2017, Andrea Thomas, https://www.wsj.com/articles/german-trial-reveals-details-of-spy-case-authorities-link-to-iran-1491989454

97   "Pakistani Man Jailed In Germany For Spying For Iran", March 28, 2017, https://www.rferl.org/a/germany-jails-pakistani-spying-iran/28396497.html

98   "Raids across Germany target suspected Iranian spies", Deutsche Welle, January 16, 2018, https://www.dw.com/en/raids-across-germany-target-suspected-iranian-spies/a-42165145

99   "Iranian resistance leader assassinated in Rome," UPI, March 16, 1993, https://www.upi.com/Archives/1993/03/16/Iranian-resistance-leader-assassinated-in-Rome/2168732258000/

100   "Iranian diplomat rejected by US implicated in Italian murder, The Telegraph, April 9, 2014, Damien McElroy, Tom Kington and Ahmed Vahdat, https://www.telegraph.co.uk/news/worldnews/middleeast/iran/10755831/Iranian-diplomat-rejected-by-US-implicated-in-Italian-murder.html

101   "Iran's UN ambassador pick accused in political assassination," FoxNews.com, April 10, 2014, http://www.foxnews.com/world/2014/04/10/iran-un-ambassador-pick-accused-in-political-assassination.html

102   Khabaronline.com, October 7, 2013

103   "House votes to bar Iran's proposed U.N. ambassador," Chicago Tribune, April 10, 2014, https://www.chicagotribune.com/.../ct-xpm-2014-04-10-sns-rt-us-iran-un-envoy-usa-...

104 "Iran Opposition Figure Killed in Rome; Exiles Blame Tehran," Los Angeles Times, March 17, 1993, William Montalbano, http://articles.latimes.com/1993-03-17/news/mn-11950_1_iranian-opposition-group

105 "Iranian diplomat rejected by US implicated in Italian murder," Daily Telegraph, April 9, 2014, Damien McElroy, Tom Kington and Ahmed Vahdat, https://www.telegraph.co.uk/news/worldnews/middleeast/iran/10755831/Iranian-diplomat-rejected-by-US-implicated-in-Italian-murder.html

106 Opcit

107 From the ruling of the Rome Criminal Appeal Court on the assassination of Mohammad Hossein Naghdi, December 18, 2008

108 "Killing of Iranian dissenters: Bloody trail back to Tehran", Washington Post, November 21, 1993, Rick Atkinson, https://www.washingtonpost.com/archive/politics/1993/11/21/killing-of-iranian-dissenters-bloody-trail-back-to-tehran/0a28474b-9ab1-485f-9949-fc18882fa909/?utm_term=.fd825d9649e5

109 Annual Report of Swedish Security service, 2008, page 23, http://www.sakerhetspolisen.se/download/18.4f0385ee143058a61a89f5/1392294914038/swedish_security_2008.pdf

110 Iran kicks out Swedish diplomat, The Local, https://www.thelocal.se/20080306/10308

111 "Iranian exiles accuse Rafsanjani of directing terrorism, killings abroad", Washington Post, April 27, 1990, George Lardner, https://www.washingtonpost.com/archive/politics/1990/04/27/iranian-exiles-accuse-rafsanjani-of-directing-terrorism-killings-abroad/610b5599-06de-4955-a240-59183dc16d2b

112 "The Tehran Connection", Time Magazine, March 21, 1994, Thomas Sancton, http://content.time.com/time/magazine/article/0,9171,164031,00.html

113 The International Herald Tribune, November 22, 1993

114   "Killing of Iranian dissenters: 'Bloody trail back to Tehran", Washington Post, November 21, 1993, Rick Atkinson, https://www.washingtonpost.com/archive/politics/1993/11/21/killing-of-iranian-dissenters-bloody-trail-back-to-tehran/0a28474b-9ab1-485f-9949-fc18882fa909

115   "Iran: State of Terror, An Account of terrorist assassinations by Iranian agents", Parliamentary Human Rights Group of the UK Parliament, London, June 1996- Page 43

116   "Le chef de la délégation iranienne attendu au Conseil des droits de l'homme était proche du commando qui a tué Kazem Radjavi," Tribune de Geneva, March 1, 2013, Alain Jourdan, https://www.tdg.ch/monde/asie-oceanie/Un-diplomate-iranien-au-passe-trouble/story/21772993

117   "Swiss orders arrest of Iranian ex-minister," Swissinfo, April 9, 2006, https://www.swissinfo.ch/eng/swiss-orders-arrest-of-iranian-ex-minister/5116960

118   Alireza Jafarzadeh (2008) . The Iran Threat: President Ahmadinejad and the Coming Nuclear Crisis. Palgrave Macmillan. p. XViii. ISBN 978-0230601284.

119   "Killing of Iranian dissenters: Bloody trail back to Tehran", Washington Post, November 21, 1993, Rick Atkinson, https://www.washingtonpost.com/archive/politics/1993/11/21/killing-of-iranian-dissenters-bloody-trail-back-to-tehran/0a28474b-9ab1-485f-9949-fc18882fa909

120   Agance France Presse, October 28, 1996.

121   "Once expelled from Turkey, Iran's FM makes a comeback", Iranfocus.com, November 26, 2005. https://tinyurl.com/y2zfpotw

122   Remarks of Abolhassan Mojtahedzadeh at a conference at the European Parliament, February 20, 2006.

123   "Iransk minister politianmeldt efter besøg i København", Politiken, May 10, 2007, Line Prasz, https://tinyurl.com/y5v2sean

124 "Iran pulls out Turkish envoy over Islam dispute", UPI, April 4, 1989, Ralph Joseph, https://www.upi.com/Archives/1989/04/04/Iran-pulls-out-Turkish-enovy-over-Islam-dispute/4404607665600/

125 "Iranian Terror on European Soil", Wall street Journal, July 23, 2018, Hossein Abedini, https://www.wsj.com/articles/iranian-terror-on-european-soil-1532386965

126 "Iran: Amnesty International concerned at reports of abduction of Iranian national on Turkey", Amnesty International, Urgent Action- June 12, 1992

127 "Terrorists trained in Iran, Minister says," Associated Press, February 4, 1993, Ahmet Balan.

128 Press release, the People's Mojahedin Organization of Iran, Paris, February 5, 1993.

129 Iran: Select Europe- Based Operational Activity, 1979-2018, Fact sheet of the US Department of State on the Iranian terrorism in Europe, complied by the National Counterterrorsim Center, July 5, 2018.

130 "Iran: State of Terror, An Account of terrorist assassinations by Iranian agents", Parliamentary Human Rights Group of the UK Parliament, London, June 1996

131 "Iran's foreign policy: kill dissidents abroad, Teheran uses hit squads as vote-catchers," The Sunday Telegraph, February 25, 1996, Con Coughlin

132 "Dissidents accuse Iran envoy of killing exiles", Reuters, February 29, 1996.

133 "Iran: State of Terror, An Account of terrorist assassinations by Iranian agents", Parliamentary Human Rights Group of the UK Parliament, London, June 1996

134 "Exiled Iranian TV Executive Is Assassinated in Istanbul", The New York Times, April 30, 2017, Patrick Kingsley, https://www.nytimes.com/2017/04/30/world/europe/saeed-karimian-iran-turkey-gem-tv.html

135 Iran sees Iraq talks this week, US says no date set, March 5, 2008, https://www.reuters.com/article/idUSL05783407

136 State-run Mehr news agency, August 28, 2016.

137 Report on the role of the regime's foreign embassies, September 2018.

138 NCRI press conference, August 25, 2018.

139 Mehr news agency, Hamedan, December 7, 2014.

140 State-run ISNA news agency, July 7, 2016. [FARSI]. <https://www.isna.ir/news/95040109290/>

141 State-run Mellat House news agency, September 12, 2018.

142 https://www.treasury.gov/resource-center/sanctions/OFAC-Enforcement/ Pages/20130530.aspx

143 Treasury Designates Iranian Ministry of Intelligence and Security for Human Rights Abuses and Support for Terrorism, February 16, 2012; https://www.treasury.gov/press-center/press-releases/Pages/tg1424.aspx

List of Publications

List of Publications by the National Council of Resistance of Iran, U.S. Representative Office

Iran Doubles Down on Terror and Turmoil

November 2018, 63 pages

This book examines the regime's political and economic strategy, which revolves around terrorism and physical annihilation of opponents. Failing to quell growing popular protests, Tehran has bolstered domestic suppression with blatant terrorism and intimidation.

Iran Will Be Free:

Speech by Maryam Rajavi

September 2018, 54 pages

This manuscript contains delivered keynote speech by Mrs. Maryam Rajavi, on June 30, 2018, at the Iranian Resistance's grand gathering in Paris, France explaining the path to freedom in Iran and what she envisions for future Iran.

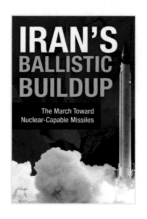

Iran's Ballistic Buildup: The March Toward Nuclear-Capable Missiles
May 2018, 136 pages

This manuscript surveys Iran's missile capabilities, including the underlying organization, structure, production, and development infrastructure, as well as launch facilities and the command centers. The book exposes the nexus between the regime's missile activities and its nuclear weapons program, including ties with North Korea.

Iran: Cyber Repression: How the IRGC Uses Cyberwarfare to Preserve the Theocracy
February 2018, 70 pages

This manuscript demonstrates how the Iranian regime, under the supervision and guidance of the IRGC and the Ministry of Intelligence and Security (MOIS), have employed new cyberwarfare and tactics in a desperate attempt to counter the growing dissent inside the country.

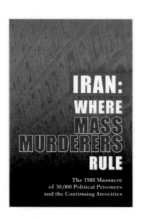

Iran: Where Mass Murderers Rule: The 1988 Massacre of 30,000 Political Prisoners and the Continuing Atrocities
November 2017, 161 pages

Iran: Where Mass Murderers Rule is an expose of the current rulers of Iran and their track record in human rights violations. The book details how 30,000 political prisoners fell victim to politicide during the summer of 1988 and showcases the egregious political extinction of a group of people.

Iran's Nuclear Core: Uninspected Military Sites, Vital to the Nuclear Weapons Program

October 2017, 52 pages

This book details how the nuclear weapons program is at the heart of, and not parallel to, the civil nuclear program of Iran. The program has been run by the Islamic Revolutionary Guards Corp (IRGC) since the beginning, and the main nuclear sites and nuclear research facilities have been hidden from the eyes of the United Nations nuclear watchdog.

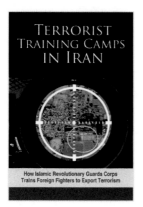

Terrorist Training Camps in Iran: How Islamic Revolutionary Guards Corps Trains Foreign Fighters to Export Terrorism

June 2017, 56 pages

The book details how Islamic Revolutionary Guards Corps trains foreign fighters in 15 various camps in Iran to export terrorism. The IRGC has created a large directorate within its extraterritorial arm, the Quds Force, in order to expand its training of foreign mercenaries as part of the strategy to step up its meddling abroad in Syria, Iraq, Yemen, Bahrain, Afghanistan and elsewhere.

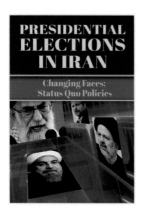

Presidential Elections in Iran: Changing Faces; Status Quo Policies

May 2017, 78 pages

The book reviews the past 11 presidential elections, demonstrating that the only criterion for qualifying as a candidate is practical and heartfelt allegiance to the Supreme Leader. An unelected vetting watchdog, the Guardian Council makes that determination.

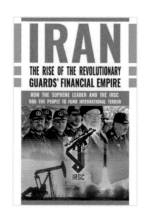

The Rise of Iran's Revolutionary Guards' Financial Empire: How the Supreme Leader and the IRGC Rob the People to Fund International Terror
March 2017, 174 pages

This manuscript examines some vital factors and trends, including the overwhelming and accelerating influence (especially since 2005) of the Supreme Leader and the Islamic Revolutionary Guard Corps (IRGC). This study shows how ownership of property in various spheres of the economy is gradually shifted from the population writ large towards a minority ruling elite comprised of the Supreme Leader's office and the IRGC, using 14 powerhouses, and how the money ends up funding terrorism worldwide.

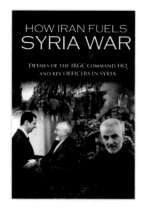

How Iran Fuels Syria War: Details of the IRGC Command HQ and Key Officers in Syria
November 2016, 74 pages

This book examines how the Iranian regime has effectively engaged in the military occupation of Syria by marshaling 70,000 forces, including the Islamic Revolutionary Guard Corps (IRGC) and mercenaries from other countries into Syria; is paying monthly salaries to over 250,000 militias and agents to prolong the conflict; and divided the country into 5 zones of conflict, establishing 18 command, logistics and operations centers.

Nowruz 2016 with the Iranian Resistance: Hoping for a New Day, Freedom and Democracy in Iran

April 2016, 36 pages

This book describes Iranian New Year, Nowruz celebrations at the Washington office of Iran's parliament-in-exile, the National Council of Resistance of Iran. The yearly event marks the beginning of spring. It includes select speeches by dignitaries who have attended the NCRIUS Nowruz celebrations. This book also discusses the very rich culture and the traditions associated with Nowruz for centuries.

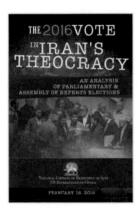

The 2016 Vote in Iran's Theocracy: An analysis of Parliamentary & Assembly of Experts Elections

February 2016, 70 pages

This book examines all the relevant data about the 2016 Assembly of Experts as well as Parliamentary elections ahead of the February 2016 elections. It looks at the history of elections since the revolution in 1979 and highlights the current intensified infighting among the various factions of the Iranian regime.

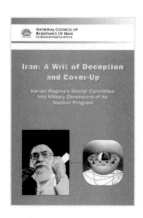

IRAN: A Writ of Deception and Cover-up: Iranian Regime's Secret Committee Hid Military Dimensions of its Nuclear Program
February 2016, 30 pages

The book provides details about a top-secret committee in charge of forging the answers to the International Atomic Energy Agency (IAEA) regarding the Possible Military Dimensions (PMD) of Tehran's nuclear program, including those related to the explosive detonators called EBW (Exploding Bridge Wire) detonator, which is an integral part of a program to develop an implosion type nuclear device.

Key to Countering Islamic Fundamentalism: Maryam Rajavi? Testimony To The U.S. House Foreign Affairs Committee
June 2015, 68 pages

Testimony before U.S. House Foreign Affairs Committee's subcommittee on Terrorism, non-Proliferation, and Trade discussing ISIS and Islamic fundamentalism. The book contains Maryam Rajavi's full testimony as well as the question and answer by representatives.

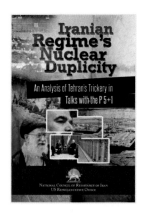

Iranian Regime's Nuclear Duplicity:
An Analysis of Tehran's Trickery in Talks with the P 5+1

January 2016, 74 pages

This book examines Iran's behavior throughout the negotiations process in an effort to inform the current dialogue on a potential agreement. Drawing on both publicly available sources and those within Iran, the book focuses on two major periods of intense negotiations with the regime: 2003-2004 and 2013-2015. Based on this evidence, it then extracts the principles and motivations behind Tehran's approach to negotiations as well as the tactics used to trick its counterparts and reach its objectives.

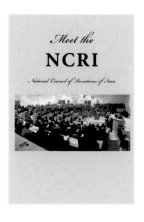

Meet the National Council of Resistance of Iran

June 2014, 150 pages

Meet the National Council of Resistance of Iran discusses what NCRI stands for, what its platform is, and why a vision for a free, democratic, secular, non-nuclear republic in Iran would serve world peace.

How Iran Regime Cheated the World:
Tehran's Systematic Efforts to Cover Up its Nuclear Weapons Program

June 2014, 50 pages

This book deals with one of the most fundamental challenges that goes to the heart of the dispute regarding the Iranian regime's controversial nuclear program: to ascertain with certainty that Tehran will not pursue a nuclear bomb. Such an assurance can only be obtained through specific steps taken by Tehran in response to the international community's concerns. The monograph discusses the Iranian regime's report card as far as it relates to being transparent when addressing the international community's concerns about the true nature and the ultimate purpose of its nuclear program

About the NCRI-US

The National Council of Resistance of Iran-US Representative Office (NCRI-US) acts as the Washington office for Iran's parliament-in-exile, the National Council of Resistance of Iran, which is dedicated to the establishment of a democratic, secular, non-nuclear republic in Iran.

NCRI-US, registered as a non-profit tax-exempt organization, has been instrumental in exposing the nuclear weapons program of Iran, including the sites in Natanz, and Arak, the biological and chemical weapons program of Iran, as well as its ambitious ballistic missile program.

NCRI-US has also exposed the terrorist network of the regime, including its involvement in the bombing of Khobar Towers in Saudi Arabia, the Jewish Community Center in Argentina, its fueling of sectarian violence in Iraq and Syria, and its malign activities in other parts of the Middle East.

Our office has provided information on the human rights violations in Iran, extensive anti-government demonstrations, and the movement for democratic change in Iran.

44160233R00108

Made in the USA
Middletown, DE
03 May 2019